ALL THE PAINTINGS OF
TITIAN

Part 4
VOLUME THIRTY-TWO
in the
Complete Library of World Art

The Complete Library of World Ar

ALL THE PAINTINGS

OF **TITIAN**

Part 4 (1546-1576)

Text by FRANCESCO VALCANOVER

Translated from the Italian by
SYLVIA J. TOMALIN

HAWTHORN BOOKS, INC.
Publishers · New York

Printed and bound in Great Britain by Jarrold and Sons Ltd, Norwich

CONTENTS

DISTRIBUTION OF PLATES

1488–1545 (*Part 1*) *Plates 1–93*
(*Part 2*) *Plates 94–223*
1546–1576 (*Part 3*) *Plates 1–111*
(*Part 4*) *Plates 112–198*

TITIAN'S PAINTINGS *continued*

Color Plate I
THE ENTOMBMENT (detail of plate 7).

Plate 112
ST MARY MAGDALENE. *Canvas, 119 × 98. Leningrad, Hermitage.* Signed: TITIANVS P. Purchased in 1850 from the Barbarigo Palace where it was taken in 1581 as part of Titian's estate. Generally dated about 1565, it is certainly the best of the many versions based on the painting sent to Spain in 1561—which itself was a replica, according to Vasari, of that originally promised to Philip II and then sold instead to Silvio Badoer of Venice (Tietze). Cf. Lost Paintings, 1561, *St Mary Magdalene.*

Plate 113
ST MARGARET AND THE DRAGON. *Canvas, 242 × 182. Madrid, Prado.* Signed: TITIANVS. This is a version, with variations, of the painting sent to Philip II in 1552 and now in the Escorial (plate 52) and may be dated about 1565 (Gronau, Pallucchini, Tietze). Mayer (1938) identifies the Prado painting with one in Charles I's Collection which was later sent to Spain. Beroqui (1946) rejects this identification.

Plate 114
VENUS BLINDFOLDING CUPID (or, THE EDUCATION OF CUPID). *Canvas, 118 × 185. Rome, Borghese Gallery.* Probably purchased by Scipione Borghese in 1608 from Cardinal Sfondrato. In the seventeenth- and eighteenth-century inventories it is listed as: "The Three Graces"; Cavalcaselle calls it "Venus Blindfolding Cupid," as does Suida (1952) who considers it to be a replica with variations of the picture in the Kress Collection in the Washington National Gallery of Art (cf. plate 176, Attributed Paintings). Valentiner (1930) names it "Cupid's Education" (Della Pergola, 1955). Usually dated about 1565 (A. Venturi, Tietze, Pallucchini). See also plates 115 and 116.

Plate 115
VENUS BLINDFOLDING CUPID. Detail: the two figures on the right.

Plate 116
VENUS BLINDFOLDING CUPID. Detail: the landscape.

Plate 117
JUDITH. *Canvas, 112 × 93. Detroit, Institute of Arts.* Formerly in the Cornwallis West Collection in London, and the Nicholson Collection. Made known by Borenius (1922), it is, according to Suida, a late transcription of a composition painted in 1530–40. Because of the difference in painting between the well-finished head, and the roughly painted remainder of this figure, Holofernes's head, and the Negro servant, Tietze suggests that this picture should be considered as an unfinished "model" which was taken up again by Titian's students. Pallucchini rejects this suggestion, and proposes a date of about 1565.

Plate 118

ST DOMINIC. *Canvas, 92 × 78. Rome, Borghese Gallery.* Signed: TICI-ANVS. Listed in the 1693 and 1700 inventories as a portrait of a Domini-can. Morelli doubtfully identifies it with the portrait of Titian's con-fessor (who belonged to the Order of Preachers) which Ridolfi mentions. The halo suggests St Dominic to Cavalcaselle, St Vincent Ferrer to Fogolari (1935). Fogolari's (1935) proposed dating of 1565 is generally accepted (Della Pergola, 1955).

Plate 119

CHRIST AT THE COLUMN. *Canvas, 86 × 58. Rome, Borghese Gallery.* From Lucrezia d'Este's estate it passed first to the Aldobrandini family and then to the Borghese family. Mentioned in the 1592 inventory of Lucrezia d'Este's pic-tures as a painting by Titian, it was attributed to him by A. Venturi in the 1893 Catalogue of the Gallery, by Longhi (1928), by Berenson, and by Della Pergola (1955) who moves the date of the picture from 1560 (the date suggested up until now) to the very last period of Titian's activity. Help from Titian's work-shop is a possibility.

Plate 120

ALLEGORY OF PRUDENCE. *Canvas, 75.6 × 68.6. London, private collection.* Formerly in the F. Howard Collec-tion in London. Hadeln (1924) considers it to be the cover for a portrait; Panofsky (1930) has detailed its exact meaning; Pallucchini ac-cepts the date of 1565 proposed by Tietze for its execution.

Plate 121

THE MARTYRDOM OF ST LAW-RENCE. *Canvas, 175 × 172. Escorial, Monastery of St Lawrence.* Still in its original place over the main altar of the old church in the Escorial. Begun in 1554 for Philip II, and seen by Vasari in process of being painted in 1566 in Titian's house, it was to be sent to Spain on December 2, 1567. It is a version, with variations, of the painting in the Church of the Jesuits in Venice (plate 66). Cort's 1571 engraving incorporates ele-ments from both the Venice and Escorial versions (E. von Rothschild, 1931).

Plate 122

PORTRAIT OF JACOPO STRADA. *Canvas, 125 × 95. Vienna, Kunsthis-torisches Museum.* Signed: TITIANVS F.; on the letter lying on the table is written: AL MGCO SIGOre IL SIGOr TITIAN VECELLIO . . . VENEZIA. In the Collection of the Archduke Leopold William in 1659. Begun in 1567 and completed in 1568 (H. Zimmermann, VI).

Plate 123

PORTRAIT OF JACOPO STRADA. Detail: the head.

Plate 124

THE ENTOMBMENT. *Canvas, 130 × 168. Madrid, Prado.* Signed: TITIANVS F. May most probably be identified with the painting noted in Titian's house in 1566 by Vasari (Ricketts, 1910; Rothschild, 1931). Cavalcaselle believed it to be an imitation by a Spanish painter, but R. Longhi (1925) quite rightly re-attributed it to Titian and suggested a dating of 1570, which Rothschild (1931) puts back to about 1566, followed by Tietze and Pallucchini. Suida (1943) considers as an authen-tic Titian the late replica (Caval-caselle) in the Ambrosiana which is mentioned in the donation docu-ments of Cardinal Federigo Borro-meo to the Ambrosiana dated April

28, 1618 (A. Ratti, *Guida somaria della Biblioteca e Collezioni annesse,* Milan, 1907).

Plate 125
MADONNA AND CHILD BETWEEN SS TITIAN AND ANDREW. *Canvas, 100 × 140. Pieve di Cadore, Archdiaconate.* This painting is identifiable with the votive picture Vasari mentions as having been painted by Titian for the chapel of the Vecellio family. Tradition has it that several members of this family are portrayed in the painting: Francesco in St Andrew, Marco in St Titian, and Titian himself in the first figure on the left with the crozier. This last identification, however, is the only plausible one. With the exception of A. Venturi (1927), all art critics in recent comment have followed Cavalcaselle in seeing the fairly extensive participation of Titian's workshop in this picture. After its restoration on the occasion of the "Exhibition of the Vecellio family" in Belluno in 1951, the canvas appears to be quite definitely an authentic Titian, datable in the late 1570's and close to the *Madonna and Child* in the National Gallery, London, reproduced here as plate 139 (F. Valcanover, 1951; Pallucchini).

Plate 126
THE TRIBUTE MONEY. *Canvas, 109 × 101.5. London, National Gallery.* Signed: TITIANVS F. May probably be identified with the painting sent to Philip II in Spain in 1568. Recorded in the Sacristy of the Escorial in 1657 and 1764 (W. Ximenes, *Descripción ... de l'Escorial*). This is one of the six pictures from the Spanish Royal Collection taken to France to Marshal Soult by Joseph Bonaparte (C. Gould, 1959). Cavalcaselle attributes it to Palma Giovane; Tietze believes it was

painted by Titian's workshop; Suida and Pallucchini are among those who consider it to be an authentic Titian. X-ray examination has revealed some changes during painting, particularly in the face of Christ (C. Gould, 1959).

Color Plate II
SELF-PORTRAIT (detail of plate 128).

Plate 127
CHRIST CARRYING THE CROSS. *Canvas, 67 × 77. Madrid, Prado.* Signed: TITIANVS AEQ. CAES. F. Listed for the first time in the 1666 inventory (Beroqui, 1946). Wickhoff attributes it to Palma Giovane, but most critics consider it a genuine Titian. Fischel and Tietze date it to 1560, Suida to about 1570, Pallucchini to between 1565 and 1570.

Plate 128
SELF-PORTRAIT. *Canvas, 86 × 65. Madrid, Prado.* Listed for the first time in the March 1666 inventory (Beroqui, 1946). Suida dates the painting after 1562, followed by Tietze and Pallucchini, who notes the facial resemblance with the portrait of Titian engraved by Cort in 1567 from *The Adoration of the Holy Trinity* painted for Charles V (plate 53). The identification of this Prado canvas with the self-portrait Vasari saw in Titian's house has no foundation in fact; this latter picture is probably the one in the Berlin Museum (plate 98).

Plate 129
THE FALL OF MAN. *Canvas 290 × 186. Madrid, Prado.* Signed: TITIANVS F. Mentioned for the first time in the Chapel of the Alcazar in Madrid, and damaged in the 1734 fire there; afterwards it was restored and extensively repainted by Don Juán

de Miranda. It has been variously dated between 1560 and 1570—the later date being the most plausible (Gronau, Tietze), even if art critics agree that Titian had a much earlier prototype in mind when he painted it. Indeed, Pallucchini puts forward the hypothesis that the artist put the finishing touches between 1560 and 1570 to a canvas begun several decades earlier.

Plate 130

SPAIN COMING TO THE AID OF RELIGION. *Canvas, 168 × 168. Madrid, Prado.* Signed: TITIANVS F. Can probably be identified with the painting representing "the triumph of Virtue over Vice" which was begun for Alfonso I d'Este, Duke of Ferrara, and left unfinished because of the duke's death in 1534. It remained in Titian's studio and was described there by Vasari in 1566. It was probably completed for Philip II after 1571 and transformed into the allegory of Spain coming to the rescue of Religion (R. Witt-kower, 1939–40). The picture was sent to Spain in 1575, and was restored there in 1625 by Vincente Carducho (J. Morena Villa, 1933). The replica in the Doria Gallery (plate 185, Attributed Paintings) which is generally considered to have been painted by Titian's workshop, is—according to Tietze-Conrat (1951)—the painting started for Alfonso I which remained in Titian's studio and which served as a model for other versions, including that in the Prado and another mentioned as being in the possession of Maximilian II which has now disappeared.

Plate 131

PHILIP II OFFERING THE INFANTE DON FERNANDO TO VICTORY. *Canvas, 335 × 274. Madrid, Prado.* Signed: TITIANVS VECELLIVS

EQES CAESARIS FECIT. Commissioned in 1571 as a memento of the Battle of Lepanto on October 7 of that year. It was being worked on in 1573 (Agatone's letter to the Duke of Urbino dated May 9, 1573; Gronau, 1904 and 1936), and was sent to Spain with the preceding picture (plate 130) in 1575. According to Moreno Villa (1933), the slave in chains was added by Carducho, who in 1625 was given the job of enlarging and restoring the painting. Although the original painting is largely hidden under this restoration, Tietze feels that the canvas was mostly painted by Titian's workshop.

Plate 132

ST SEBASTIAN. *Canvas, 212 × 116. Leningrad, Hermitage.* Purchased in 1850 from the Barbarigo family, into whose possession it came in 1581 at the time of the distribution of Titian's estate. Datable 1570 or slightly later. See also plate 133.

Plate 133

ST SEBASTIAN. Detail: the bust.

Plate 134

THE CROWN OF THORNS. *Canvas, 280 × 182. Munich, Bayerische Staatsgemäldesammlungen.* Formerly in the Elector of Bavaria's gallery. It can probably be identified with the canvas Ridolfi and Boschini mention as having passed to Jacopo Tintoretto when Titian's estate was scattered, and as having been sold by Domenico Tintoretto to an "ultramontane" merchant (Von Hadeln). It is a version, dating from about 1570, of the Louvre painting (Part II, plate 170).

Plate 135

ECCE HOMO. Canvas, *110 × 93. St Louis, Art Museum.* Formerly in the Heinemann Collection, it could be—according to Tietze—the painting offered in 1640 to Bishop Coccapani in Reggio. Published by Mayer as an authentic Titian dating from 1565, it is considered as such by most critics—and also by Tietze in 1950. This critic was doubtful about the attribution in 1936. The painting may be dated about 1570. Tietze-Conrat (1946) considers it a "sketch" which remained in Titian's workshop to serve as a model for other replicas. These are numerous, and among them must be included the Prado version (cf. note to plate 183, Attributed Paintings). The copy with variations in the Wildenstein Collection was certainly painted by Pietro Vecchia.

Plate 136
TARQUIN AND LUCRETIA. *Canvas, 188.9 × 145.4. Cambridge, Fitzwilliam Museum.* Signed: "TITIANVS F." This canvas can most probably be identified with the picture that Titian assured Philip II in a letter dated August 1, 1571, he had sent to Spain, and of which Cort made an engraving in the same year. It was still in Spain at the beginning of the nineteenth century, and then was taken to England. Its last English owner, Fairfax Murray, donated it to the Museum in 1918. Another version of this subject was preserved (F. Ingersoll Smouse, 1926) in the Museum in Bordeaux (cf. Lost Paintings, ca. 1570, *Tarquin and Lucretia*).

Plate 137
TARQUIN AND LUCRETIA. *Canvas, 140 × 100. Vienna, Gemäldegalerie der Akademie der Bildenden Kunst.* Bought in 1907 in the Schroff sale in Vienna. According to Popp (1921), this is a later reduction of the canvas which Cort engraved; Tietze thinks it may

be a preparatory sketch which Titian kept in his studio. See also plate 138.

Plate 138
TARQUIN AND LUCRETIA. Detail: Lucretia's head.

Plate 139
MADONNA AND CHILD. *Canvas, 75.6 × 63.2. London, National Gallery.* Formerly in the collections of Lord Ward (1850) and Mond in London (1924). This canvas is very close to the small votive altarpiece of Pieve di Cadore, and may be dated about 1570. The attribution to Titian of the painting in the Henniker-Heaton Collection—which Hadeln (1928) considers to be a preparatory study for this *Madonna* in the National Gallery—is quite rightly rejected by Tietze (C. Gould, 1959).

Plate 140
CHILD WITH DOGS. *Canvas, 128 × 180. Rotterdam, Boymans Museum (von Beuningen Collection).* Formerly in the Serbelloni Collection. According to Venturi (1931), this is a votive picture, but probably only part of a much larger composition (Tietze). Usually dated the last five years of Titian's activity.

Plate 141
NYMPH AND SHEPHERD. *Canvas, 142 × 187. Vienna, Kunsthistorisches Museum.* In the collection of the Archduke Leopold William in 1659. The nymph's pose brings to mind the figure in Giulio Campagnola's engraving based on a Giorgione composition. According to Gronau, it may be dated about 1565, or possibly later; Fischel dates it between 1560 and 1570; Tietze thinks it may be identified with the picture representing "Diana and Endymion," one of the paintings Titian offered to

Maximilian II in 1568. Pallucchini dates it in the early 1570s. From the copy by Palma il Giovane which Count Giustiniani di Venezia donated to the Museo Civico in Treviso (1958), it may be deduced that this Vienna painting was sliced on both sides, as Jedlicka had previously suggested (1947). See also plate 142.

Plate 142
NYMPH AND SHEPHERD. Detail: the landscape on the right.

Color Plate III
THE FALL OF MAN (detail of plate 129).

Plate 143
THE PUNISHMENT OF MARSYAS. *Canvas, 212 × 207. Kromieriz, National Gallery.* It is listed as a painting by Titian in the auction sale in 1670 in Vienna, and also in the collection of Bishop Olmutz, who purchased it in 1673. Frimmel (1909) listed it with a definite attribution to Titian, and all critics today agree that this painting is one of the artist's very last masterpieces.

Plate 144
THE DEPOSITION. *Canvas, 351 × 389. Venice, Accademia.* The inscription at the bottom reads: QUOD TITIANVS INCHOANTUM RELIQUI / PALMA REVERENTE ABSOLVIT / DEOQ. DICAVIT OPUS. In the bottom right-hand corner is the Vecellio family coat-of-arms, and a mock votive tablet with the portraits of Titian and his son Orazio praying before the Virgin. Titian painted the picture for the Chapel of the Crucifixion in the Church of the Frari where he wished to be buried; because of some differences of opinion with the monks, the canvas remained in an unfinished state in the artist's studio, was finished after his death by Palma Giovane, and was displayed in the Church of Sant' Angelo. After the church's demolition it was taken to the Accademia. During the recent restoration (1953) it has been possible to ascertain that Palma il Giovane, who painted the whole of the angel in the top part of the picture bearing a candle, did much less than a well-known passage in Boschini would lead one to suppose. See also plates 145 and 146.

Plate 145
THE DEPOSITION. Detail: Christ's head.

Plate 146
THE DEPOSITION. Detail: the statue of Moses.

Color Plate IV
SPAIN COMING TO THE AID OF RELIGION (Detail of plate 130).

LOST PAINTINGS

1545. VENUS. On December 8, 1545, Titian wrote from Rome to Charles V that he hoped personally to present him with "a figure of Venus made by me in your name" (Lafenestre, 1886, 1909; Beroqui, 1946). It is possibly the one the artist offered Charles V in 1548 (see below).

1545–46. ECCE HOMO. Described by Vasari as painted in Rome for the Farnese family: "They persuaded him to paint, to give as a present to the Pope, a Christ from the waist up, in the form of 'Ecce Homo'; this work was as though the works of Michelangelo, Raphael, Polidoro and others had made it fail, or there was some other reason, because it did not seem to the painters that it was a good work, of the same excellence as many of Titian's others, particularly the portraits."

1545–46. PORTRAIT OF GIULIA VARANA, DUCHESS OF URBINO. Noted by Pietro Aretino in a letter he wrote to the Duchess of Urbino in October 1545 (III/331), and mentioned several times in the Urbino correspondence of 1546 and 1547. According to Gronau (1936), it can be identified in the portrait in Palazzo Pitti which is otherwise justly considered by recent criticism to be a copy (cf. Attributed Paintings, *Supposed Portrait of Giulia Varana*, p. 84).

1546. PORTRAIT OF FRANCESCO DONATO. In January 1546 (III/592), Aretino wrote to Titian in Rome reminding him that he had not yet finished the portrait of Francesco Donato before he was elected Doge, and invited the artist to complete it as soon as he returned to Venice.

1546. PORTRAITS OF HENRY VIII OF ENGLAND AND HIS SON EDWARD. Aretino, in a letter dated March 1546, asked Titian to complete the undertaking.

1546. PORTRAIT OF PIETRO ARE-TINO. A replica of the portrait Titian painted for Cosimo I, taken by Francis I from the Constable of Montmorency (Aretino, letter of July 1546 to Volterra, IV/97). In 1546, Aretino promised another replica of his portrait to Giovio, who had asked him for one some time previously (IV/45).

c. 1546. ANNUNCIATION. "He painted a Virgin of the Annunciation on a small panel in the Church of Santa Maria Nuova in Venice" (Vasari).

1547. PAINTING OF AN UNIDENTI-FIED SUBJECT. Titian, in a letter of June 18, 1547, in which he asked Cardinal Alessandro Farnese for the Lead Office, reminded him that he had ready a picture, "keeping it with him, awaiting the Cardinal's wishes in the matter" (A. Ronchini, 1864).

1547. PORTRAIT OF THE DOGE FRANCESCO DONATO (1545–53). The Council of Ten decided that Titian should be recompensed for the portrait of the Doge hung in the Hall of the Grand Council (Lorenzi, 1868, 559).

1547. ECCE HOMO. A replica, given by Titian to Aretino at Christmas 1547, of the painting the artist took to Augsburg as a present for Charles V (plate 20). According to A. Venturi, it is to be identified in the painting in the Musée Condé of Chantilly, in which Christ holds the rod in his right hand—as described by Aretino (IV/180).

1548. DOUBLE PORTRAIT OF CHARLES V AND ISABELLA. In a list of his works painted in Augsburg in 1548 and included in his letter of September 1, 1548, to Chancellor Granvella, Titian notes also "that of His Majesty and the Empress" (M. Zarco del Valle, 1888). A copy of this double portrait exists: it is attributed to Rubens and is in the Frank Sabin Collection in London (A. Scharf, 1935), and is reproduced here as plate 193.

1548. PORTRAIT OF FERDINAND I. In the portrait painted in 1548 in Augsburg (Aretino, V/518; Vasari), the king was represented "in armor, but without helmet" (A. Pinchart, 1856). It cannot, therefore, be identified with the Naples portrait (see note to plate 155a).

1548. VENUS. Noted by Titian as completed for Charles V in his letter to Granvella dated September 1, 1548 (M. R. Zarco del Valle, 1888).

1548. ECCE HOMO. On 23 (October?) 1548, Titian mentions to Nicolas Granvella among other things: "Your Excellency can keep the *Christ* until I come to Italy and can paint another in greater comfort" (M. R. Zarco del Valle, 1888).

1548. PORTRAIT OF MARIE, QUEEN OF HUNGARY and sister of Charles V. Painted in Augsburg, it is listed as No. 5 in the Queen's own inventory in 1556 (A. Pinchart, 1856). A copy (86 × 65) of the portrait is in the Musée des Arts Décoratifs in Paris (G. Glück, 1934).

1548. PORTRAIT OF CHRISTINA OF DENMARK, Duchess of Lorraine and wife of Francesco Sforza, Duke of Milan. It is listed as No. 7 in the 1556 inventory of Queen Marie of Hungary (A. Pinchart, 1856).

1548. PORTRAIT OF MARIE JACQUELINE OF BADEN, widow of William I of Bavaria. Two portraits of the Duchess are listed as Nos. 8 and 14 in the 1556 inventory of Queen Marie of Hungary (A. Pinchart, 1856).

1548. PORTRAIT OF JOHN FREDERICK OF SAXONY, IN ARMOR. Mentioned by Vasari and by Cesare Vecellio (1590), it is probably the painting listed as No. 9 in the 1556 inventory of Queen Marie of Hungary (A. Pinchart, 1856). A copy of it exists in the Prado (plate 194). No. 10 of the same inventory is listed as another portrait of Charles V's famous prisoner, without armor this time; however, it is not possible to identify this painting definitely with that in the Kunsthistorisches Museum in Vienna (see note to plate 29, Part III).

1548. PORTRAIT OF MAURICE OF SAXONY. Listed as No. 11 in the 1556 inventory of Queen Marie of Hungary (A. Pinchart, 1856).

1548. PORTRAIT OF DOROTHY, wife of Frederick II of Pfalz. Listed as No. 12 in the 1556 inventory of Queen Marie of Hungary (A. Pinchart, 1856).

1548. PORTRAIT OF MAXIMILIAN, KING OF BOHEMIA, and son of Ferdinand I. Painted in Augsburg in 1548 and mentioned by Vasari. In the 1556 inventory of the pictures of Queen Marie of Hungary, a portrait of Maximilian is in fact listed as No. 15 (A. Pinchart, 1856).

1548. PORTRAIT OF EMANUELE FILIBERTO OF SAVOIA. Noted by Vasari, it is listed as No. 16 in Queen Marie of Hungary's inventory in 1556 (A. Pinchart, 1856).

1548. PORTRAIT OF THE ARCH-DUKE FERDINAND, son of Ferdinand I. Mentioned by Vasari as having been painted in Augsburg in 1548, it is probably the one listed as No. 23 in the 1556 inventory of Queen Marie of Hungary (A. Pinchart, 1856).

1548. PORTRAITS OF THE DAUGH-TERS OF FERDINAND I. Noted by Vasari and by Aretino (V/518). In his letter from Innsbruck of October 20, 1548, to Ferdinand, Titian mentions that he has to finish these portraits in Venice (D. von Hadeln, 1914). In the inventory of Queen Marie of Hungary, Nos. 27–30 are listed as portraits of the four daughters of Ferdinand, painted by Titian. The portrait of Ferdinand's daughters noted by Cavalcaselle in the Cowper Collection at Panshanger in England is by Titian's school.

1548–49. PORTRAIT OF PRINCE PHILIP. Painted in Milan during Philip's brief stay there between December 20, 1548, and January 7, 1549 (M. R. Zarzo del Valle, 1888). See note to plate 42.

1548–54. ECCE HOMO; PORTRAIT OF PHILIP; VARIOUS PAINTINGS. The *Ecce Homo* which Titian prom-ised Nicolas Granvella on (October?) 23, 1548, was sent off by him before April 28, 1549, as is shown by a letter of this date, in which Granvella con-veys to the artist his wish "to have a portrait of the Prince our master, which you painted in Milan." This replica was finished by Titian in 1550 and sent off on March 22 of the same year to Granvella (M. R. Zarco del Valle, 1888). As is also shown by the correspondence between Titian and Granvella during the period 1548–54, Titian must have executed many paintings for Charles V's powerful Chancellor. In fact, one of his grand-children, François de Granvelle, Count of Contecroix, sold to Rudolf II, together with many other works of art from his grandfather's vast collection, "A picture on canvas of a Venus in her bed, with an organist" (cf. note to plate 32) and "a picture on canvas of a sleeping Venus with a hidden satyr," both by Titian (*Jahrbuch Viennese,* 1888, R.4656 and R.4634). As well, he left to his heirs a group of Titian's paintings which included, besides the portraits of Nicolas Granvella (two versions) and his wife Nicoline Bonvalot, a "Venus at her mirror which is held by a Cupid," a "Woman wearing a chemise," an "Enormous head," and a "Boy" (Cavalcaselle, with bibliography).

1549. PORTRAIT OF LAVINIA RANGONE. Augustina Rangone ask-ed Titian in 1549 to finish the por-trait of her daughter Lavinia.

1549. PORTRAIT OF THE DUKE OF ALBA. Mentioned by Aretino in a letter, accompanied by a sonnet, to the Duke in March 1549 (V/219). Listed as No. 26 in the 1556 inven-tory of Queen Marie of Hungary. The portrait of the Duke in the possession of the heirs of the D'Alba family in Madrid is thought by some scholars to be an original replica (C. Justi, 1889; A. L. Mayer, 1938).

1549. PORTRAIT OF GIULIANO GOSELLINI. According to Pietro Aretino, Titian painted the portrait of Gonzaga's secretary in order to obtain payment of his pension (letter to the Duke of Alba, V/105).

1549. PORTRAITS. On January 29, 1549, Prince Philip ordered Domingo de Orbea, Master of the Palace of Charles V, to pay Titian a thousand gold *scudi* "for some portraits which he has sent me" (R. Beer, 1891).

1549. PORTRAIT OF QUEEN MARIE OF HUNGARY. Noted by Granvella in his letter to Titian of June 21, 1549 (M. R. Zarzo del Valle, 1888). Possibly a replica of the portrait of the queen painted in Augsburg in 1548.

1549. PORTRAIT OF CATHERINE OF AUSTRIA, wife of Francesco, Duke of Mantua. Mentioned in a letter dated June 21, 1549, from the Mantuan ambassador, Agnelli, to the Duke of Mantua (Luzio, 1884).

1549. PORTRAIT OF CHARLES V. Replica of the Emperor's portrait for the Duke of Mantua, mentioned by Titian in a letter he wrote in September 1549 to Ferrante Gonzaga (Cavalcaselle). Some scholars identify it with the supposed portrait of Ferdinand in Capodimonte in Naples (plate 155a).

1549. PORTRAIT OF PIETRO ARETINO. In a letter written in September 1549, Aretino promised Gregorio Ricoveri "a copy" of his own portrait painted by Titian in 1545.

1549. TANTALUS. One of the paintings in the series known as "of the Furies" or "of the Damned," commissioned from Titian in 1548 by Queen Marie of Hungary. There is a record of this painting in the engraving by Sanudo, given here as plate 195. According to Tietze, a fourth picture of this series, representing Ixion and mentioned in the 1558 inventory of Simancas (C. Justi, 1889; A. Beer, 1891), was sent to Flanders in 1553, but there are no known copies or graphic transcriptions of it (cf. note to plate 30 Part III). It is, in any case, highly doubtful whether it was painted by Titian (Beroqui, 1946).

1550. SELF-PORTRAIT. See, in Attributed Paintings (page 86), the *Self-Portrait* formerly in Berlin in the Von Kaufmann Collection.

1550. PORTRAIT OF CHARLES V. Commissioned by the Emperor through Leoni, to send to the "most illustrious Princess of Spain," it was sent on March 22, 1550 (M. Zarco del Valle, 1888).

1550. PORTRAIT OF PHILIP. Sent to Granvella on March 22, 1550, together with a replica for this same Bishop of Arras (M. R. Zarco del Valle, 1888; see also under 1548–54, *Portrait of Philip*).

1551–53. PORTRAITS; MARY MAGDALENE. Mentioned in a letter dated August 4, 1553, from Francesco Vargas to Marie of Hungary.

Before 1552. UNIDENTIFIED SUBJECTS; STRUGGLE; ECCE HOMO. TWO FEMALE PORTRAITS. In the inventory of works of art collected by Gabriele Vendramin (who died in 1552), drawn up by Tommaso da Lugano, Jacopo Sansovino, Alessandro Vittoria, Jacopo Tintoretto and Orazio Vecellio between 1567 and 1569, several paintings by Titian are mentioned, apart from the London portrait of Vendramin and the artist's self-portrait (see under the year 1550 in this list): on August 26, 1567, "all these things," vases, small marbles, etc., "were . . . painted by the hand of Messer Titian"; on September 10, 1567, "A small painting of a man in armor with a boy . . ., by the hand of Ser Titian with the small painting of the wedding at Cana"—and this is possibly the painting seen by Michiel in the Venier house in 1528; on March 14, 1569, "A Christ with two figures, one either side, by the hand of Messer Titian together with the inlaid golden frame"—to be identified, according to Gronau, with the Louvre picture given here as plate 158; "A portrait of a gentlewoman by the hand of Messer Titian together with a decorated golden frame"; "Another portrait of a gentlewoman by the hand of Ser Titian together with a differently decorated golden frame" (A. Ravà, 1920).

1552. PORTRAIT OF GUIDOBALDO II. Mentioned by the Duke of Urbino in two of his letters, dated February 22 and May 10, 1552, to Leonardi (Gronau, 1936).

1552. PORTRAIT OF THE DUKE OF ATRI. Pietro Aretino, in a letter written to the Duke of Atri in August 1552 (VI/290), praised the portrait of the Duke painted by Titian. The identification of this picture with the Kassel one (plate 40, Part 3) is uncertain.

1552. SELF-PORTRAIT. Sent to Philip II by Vasari on October 11, 1552. Noted in Palazzo del Pardo in 1564, it was probably destroyed in the 1604 fire (Beroqui, 1946).

1552. QUEEN OF PERSIA; LANDSCAPE; ST MARGARET. These three paintings are mentioned in Titian's letter to Philip II dated October 11, 1552 (Simancas Archives, Cavalcaselle).

1552. CHRIST. In a letter dated December 12, 1552, Guidobaldo II begged Leonardi to urge Titian into finishing a *Christ* (Gronau, 1936).

1553. PORTRAIT OF PHILIP II. Replica with variations of the full-length portrait of the king, which Philip thanked the artist for sending to Spain in his letter of June 18, 1553 (Simancas Archives, Cavalcaselle). Some scholars identify it with the Naples painting (see note to plate 48).

1553–54. PORTRAIT OF FRANCESCO VARGAS, Charles V's ambassador to Venice. Mentioned in one of Aretino's letters in October 1553 (VI/290), it is also noted in Titian's letter dated September 10, 1554, to Charles V.

1553–54. NOLI ME TANGERE. Painted for Queen Marie of Hungary and seen by Ambassador Vargas in 1553 in Titian's studio, it was probably sent to Flanders on October 11, 1554, together with the *Holy Trinity* (plate 53, Part 3). In 1566, Philip II ordered the painting to be reduced to the bust of Christ only (plate 54, Part 3) which entered the Escorial in 1574 (Salazar catalogue, 1949). A record of the composition as a whole is to be found in the copy attributed to A. S. Coello in the Escorial, reproduced here as plate 196.

1554. PORTRAIT OF THOMAS PERRENOT GRANVELLA. Mentioned as still being in Titian's studio in a letter written by Aretino in January 1554 (VI/338).

1554. PORTRAIT OF THE DOGE
MARCANTONIO TREVISAN (1553–
54). On February 28, 1554, the
Council of Ten gave the order to
recompense Titian for his portrait
of the Doge painted for the Hall of
the Grand Council (Lorenzi, 1868,
602). Aretino also mentioned the
portrait in a letter written in November 1553 to Boccamazza (VI/203).
It was destroyed in the 1577 fire.
Cavalcaselle notes a copy in the
Sterne Collection in Vienna
(99 × 86), formerly in the Festetis
Collection.

1554. MARY MAGDALENE. Sent to
Nicolas Granvella on September 15,
1554 (M. R. Zarco del Valle, 1888).

1554. VENUS. In a letter to Charles V
written in December 1555 (VI/434),
Aretino mentioned how much the
Emperor had liked the "Trinity"
(The Adoration of the Holy Trinity
now in the Prado) and a "Venus"
sent by Titian to Flanders. This is
probably the "Venus and Cupid"
listed as No. 37 in the 1556 inventory
of the paintings belonging to Queen
Marie of Hungary (A. Pinchart,
1856).

1554. PORTRAIT OF FRANCESCO
VARGAS. Mentioned by Titian in his
September 10, 1554, letter to Charles
V (Simancas Archives, Office of the
Secretary of State, 1336 Leg.; Caval-
caselle).

1554–55. THE DOGE MARCAN-
TONIO TREVISAN, KNEELING BE-
FORE THE MADONNA AND CHILD,
AND BEING PRESENTED BY SS
MARK, ANTHONY, DOMINIC AND
FRANCIS. Titian undertook to
paint this votive picture on Septem-
ber 5, 1554. By January 7, 1555,
it was already "in large part finished
to perfection"; the final payment for

it was made on January 28, 1556.
It was hung "above the door of the
Sala dei Pregadi" (Lorenzi, 1868,
pp. 608, 610, 614, 629); it disappeared in the 1575 fire.

After 1554. JASON AND MEDEA and
"A very pious work." Promised by
Titian to Philip II together with the
Perseus and Andromeda which is now
in the Wallace Collection in London
—plate 89, Part 4 (Simancas
Archives, Cavalcaselle).

1555. MADONNA. Commissioned by
Philip II and mentioned more than
once in the 1555 correspondence
between Vargas, Philip II and Titian
who found it difficult to execute the
picture on slate (R. Beer, 1891, Leg.
830).

1555. PORTRAIT OF THE DOGE
FRANCESCO VENIER (1554–56).
On March 6, 1555, the Council of
Ten ordered payment to be made for
the picture of the Doge placed in the
Sala del Maggior Consiglio (Lorenzi,
1868, 617).

1555. PORTRAITS OF ALFONSO I
AND ERCOLE II. Replicas of two
portraits of the Dukes of Ferrara
painted as a commission from
Granate, as can be gathered from a
letter dated July 9, 1555, from
Girolamo Faletti, the D'Este family's
ambassador in Venice (Archives of
the State of Modena, Cavalcaselle).

c. 1555. THE LAST SUPPER. "And
then, with the help of his young
men, he executed a "Last Supper"
in the refectory of SS Giovanni and
Paolo" (Vasari). This work was
destroyed by fire on July 17, 1571,
and in 1573 was replaced by Paolo
Veronese's Supper in the House of Levi
which is now in the Accademia,
Venice. Tietze advances the theory

that it may have been the preparatory version of the painting sent to Philip II in 1564, and which is today in the Escorial (plate 105).

Before 1556. MADONNA AND CHILD. This is probably one of the pictures Charles V took with him in his retirement to Juste (A. Pinchart, 1856).

1557. DEPOSITION. Finished and sent off in 1557, this painting was lost by the postmaster of Trent (cf. Biographical Notes), as may be gathered from Philip II's letter of January 20, 1559, to the Conte di Luna, and from the correspondence between Titian and Philip II (Cavalcaselle).

Before 1558. PORTRAIT OF STANISLAUS, Charles V's court dwarf. Noted in the hall of paintings in Palazzo del Pardo in the time of Philip II. In the 1614 inventory, two portraits of Stanislaus are listed (C. Justi, 1889).

1558. STANDARD FOR THE CONFRATERNITY OF ST BERNARDINE. June 11, 1558: "A standard was made, to put on the abbey on the feastday of St Bernardine, by Titian Vecellio of Cadore, a famous painter, and it cost seventeen Venetian *scudi* as noted in the Old Register on pages 8 and 9, and is kept in our Oratory" (San Giobbe Archives, manuscript notes of Morelli and Cicogna in the copy of the *Notizie d'opere di disegno* . . . of M. Michiel in the Marciana).

After 1558. SELF-PORTRAIT with a statue of Philip II in his hand. Described in 1582 by Argote di Molina, it was also seen by Carducho before 1608 (C. Justi, 1889).

1559. PORTRAIT OF PHILIP II. Mentioned in a letter from the Duke of Urbino to Paolo Mario dated June 5, 1559 (Gronau, 1904; 1936).

1559. PORTRAIT OF "A YOUNG TURKISH OR PERSIAN GIRL." Mentioned by Titian in his letter dated June 19, 1559, to Philip II as already finished, together with the three paintings *Diana and Callisto, Diana and Actaeon,* and the *Laying of Christ in the Sepulcher* (plates 85, 84 and 79) which were sent to Spain on September 27 of the same year (Simancas Archives, Cavalcaselle).

1559–60. ADORATION OF THE MAGI. "Titian has recently painted, in a picture three cubits tall and four wide, Jesus Christ as a child in the lap of Our Lady and being adored by the Magi, with a goodly number of figures each a cubit tall; this is a most fascinating work—as is also another painting which he himself made from the first and gave to the cardinal of Ferrara, the old man" (Vasari). While the first painting, *The Kings from the East*, mentioned by Titian in his letter of April 2, 1561, to Philip II (cf. Biographical Notes) is certainly the version in the Escorial given here as plate 76 (Beroqui, 1946), the second one (which Cardinal Ippolito d'Este had in mind to offer to Henry II, King of France) is identified by some scholars with the Ambrosiana picture (plate 77), and by Tietze-Conrat (1954) with that in the Löthy Collection in Aarburg which is entirely different from all the other versions of this subject attributed to Titian (plate 170).

c. 1560. FLAGELLATION OF CHRIST. "For the Queen of Portugal he painted a picture of a very life-like Christ at the column, being whipped by the Jews, which is very beautiful" (Vasari). The model for this painting was possibly the "sketch" which Ridolfi mentions as coming to Jacopo Tintoretto together with other paintings after Titian's death: "some sketches of Christ crowned with thorns, the same being whipped at the column." The two engravings of B. Franco and of Martino Rota (the second from 1568) are possibly derived from the Queen of Portugal's picture (Tietze, Fig. 319b).

1561. ST MARY MAGDALENE. "Afterwards, Titian painted—to send to the Catholic King—a three-quarter-length figure of a St Mary Magdalene in disarray: that is to say, with her hair falling down over her shoulders, round her neck, and over her breast, while, with her head raised and her eyes fixed on heaven, she shows repentance in the redness of her eyes, and sorrow for her sins in her tears; this picture moves whoever sees it, and—what is more—although it is very beautiful, it does not provoke the onlooker's lascivious feelings but his feelings of commiseration. This picture, when it was finished, pleased Silvio, . . . a Venetian nobleman, so much that he gave Titian one hundred *scudi* in order that he might have the picture —as do those who take the highest pleasure in paintings; so that Titian was forced to paint another, which was just as beautiful, to send to the aforesaid Catholic King" (Vasari). From the correspondence between García Hernandez and Philip II it becomes clear that the painting was sent to Philip II in 1561. It is recorded in the Sacristy of the Escorial, where we now find a copy by Luca Giordano (C. Justi, 1889; Beroqui, 1946). The other version

was bought by Silvio Badoer "and after his death passed to the Elmani family, Flemish merchants, who paid five hundred *scudi* for it, and when the family left Venice it was afterwards sent to Flanders" (Ridolfi). Ridolfi also notes that he is in possession of an original replica, one of the many mentioned in the sixteenth and seventeenth centuries (in the Church of the Miracoli in Venice says Boschini; as formerly being in the possession of Rubens says Sainsbury; in the collections of Louis XIV and Louis XV claims Dam; in the possession of N. Grasso claims Ridolfi; in the Ruzzini house in Venice says Sansovino; in the Muselli house says Ridolfi; in two versions in the collection of Queen Cristina, in the collection of Ippolito Capilupi, Bishop of Fano, claims D'Arco—1857—according to Cavalcaselle's list). Among the many replicas and versions of the two lost paintings noted by Vasari which are known today, the one in Leningrad stands out because of its high quality (plate 112, and Attributed Paintings, p. 93).

1562. VENUS AND ADONIS; MADONNA. In his letter of May 24, 1562, Titian notifies Vecellio Vecelli: "Horatio sends you your small picture of Adonis, which is very beautiful, and you will enjoy it until the other one of Our Lady is attended to" (Cavalcaselle).

1562. UNIDENTIFIED SUBJECT. On April 10, 1562, García Hernandez informed Philip II that Titian was finishing a small painting for him (Simancas Archives, Cavalcaselle).

1564. PORTRAIT OF PHILIP II'S SISTER AS QUEEN OF THE ROMANS.

Sent by García Hernandez to Philip II on June 11, 1564 (Simancas Archives, Cavalcaselle).

1564–66. ECCE HOMO; MADONNA. Agatone in his letter of January 26, 1566, assured Guidobaldo, Duke of Urbino, that Titian had told him that "the two holy pictures—that is, the one of Christ and the one of the Madonna—are completed by his own hand." The *Madonna* is noted in the Urbino correspondence for the year 1564 (Gronau, 1904; 1936).

1564–68. THE FORGE OF THE CYCLOPS; BRESCIA, MINERVA AND MARS AND THREE NAIADS; CERES AND BACCHUS. These three paintings were commissioned from Titian in 1564 for the ceiling of the main hall in the town hall of Brescia decorated by Cristoforo Rosa. They were brought to Brescia by Orazio in 1568. Debate then arose over their payment, because the Brescian authorities insisted that the three canvases were not by Titian (B. Zamboni, 1778). They were destroyed in the Brescia town hall fire of January 18, 1575, but there is a record of two of them in the engraving by C. Cort (or Meyer, according to Kristeller, 1911), and in a drawing attributed to Rubens in the British Museum (E. Tietze-Conrat, 1954). The engraving and the drawing are both reproduced here, as plate 197.

c. 1566. THE CRUCIFIXION; ALLEGORY WITH MINERVA AND NEPTUNE; NOLI ME TANGERE; THE LAYING OF CHRIST IN THE SEPULCHER; MADONNA; ST PAUL. "As well as the things already mentioned, and many others of less worth which this man has painted and which are not mentioned for the sake of brevity, he has in his house the following paintings, sketched, and started . . . a large canvas depicting Christ on the cross, with the thieves and those who are crucifying them below, which he is painting for Messer Giovanni d'Anna; . . . He also began, many years ago, for Alfonso I, Duke of Ferrara, a picture of a nude young woman who curtseys to Minerva with another figure nearby, and the sea, in the midst of which Neptune appears in the distance on his cart; but because of the death of the gentleman for whom the picture was being painted, at his wish it was not finished and remained with Titian. He has also gone a good way with, but not finished, a picture in which Christ appears to Mary Magdalene in the orchard in the form of a gardener, a most life-like figure; and likewise another of a similar size in which the dead Christ is laid in the sepulcher in the presence of the Madonna and the other Marys; and a picture also of Our Lady which is one of the good things in that house; and finally a St Paul reading, a half-figure, which itself seems full of the Holy Spirit" (Vasari, from the notes he took during his visit to Titian's studio in 1566, and given in the 1568 edition of the *Lives*). While the *Crucifixion* may be identified, according to some scholars, with the painting in Bologna (plate 182), Tietze believes that the *Noli me tangere* may be the model which remained in Titian's workshop for the picture sent to Flanders in 1554 (plate 54, Part 3). The *Entombment of Christ* would seem to have been both requested and obtained in 1572 by the Spanish Prime Minister Antonio Perez (Cavalcaselle). Its identification with the *Entombment* in the Vienna Kunsthistorisches Museum is untenable because of the mediocre quality of the Vienna picture, while much more relevant stylistically is the painting, in the second version of the subject, in the Prado in Madrid (plate 124). For the painting left unfinished because of the death of Alfonso I, Duke of Ferrara, cf. notes to plates 130 and 185.

Before 1566. APOLLO; DIANA. Seen by Vasari in 1566 in Venice in the house of Gian Maria Verdizzotti: "This man has two figures painted in oils in two niches: an Apollo, and a Diana—by Titian, whom he loves and looks on as his father."

1566-67. FRESCOES IN THE CHOIR OF THE PARISH CHURCH IN PIEVE DI CADORE. In 1566, Titian agreed to arrange for the fresco painting, from his own drawings, of the choir in the Parish Church in Pieve di Cadore by his pupils, among them Valerio Zuccato, Emanuele d'Augusta and Cesare Vecellio (Cavalcaselle). These frescoes were started in 1566, and completed by 1567. The church was torn down in 1813, and a record of the frescoes remains in the description Ticozzi (1817) gives of them a few years after their destruction: "In the four central compartments of the vault, the four Evangelists were painted, life-size and with their respective symbols, above the lightest of clouds against an azure background, and in the two compartments above the altar, two most fascinating angels clothed in transparent veiling which reached just above their knees, presenting the scepter and crown to the Virgin. In the compartment opposite the altar which was joined to the great arch of the choir, another angel was to be seen in rapid movement, as would be expected of a celestial being rising to heaven with the triumphant insignia of the cross. The other two parts of the vault

formed part of the pictures to the sides. In the right-hand one, he painted a very pretty young Virgin of the Annunciation, kneeling on a footstool under a wide pavilion-like swathe of green cloth, and showing, in the sweet look in her eyes and the modest blush animating her face, the surprise of her gentle spirit upon seeing the heavenly messenger before her. . . . In the corner of the vault above, the figure of the Eternal Father loomed massively from out of the clouds, extending his arms towards the Virgin, while from the heavenly dove, representing the Holy Spirit, a beam of light flashed downwards towards her. . . . In the opposite picture the birth of Christ was represented. The pose of the Virgin and Child were exactly the same as in the manger scene of Belluno, described in the first book, p. 73, etc. [today in the Museum of Fine Arts in Houston; cf. note to Attributed Paintings in Part 2. Adoration of the Shepherds, p. 113]; but in this one the figure of St Joseph, both in pose and beauty of facial expression . . . was much superior to the other. From the left side, some shepherds were coming forward, the one leading the ox being portrayed in the most natural and picturesque pose possible. In the background, a country scene of sheep and flocks opened out, with trees most beautifully depicted in it. A glorious host of angels . . . occupied the upper part of the picture. Not to be forgotten were a St John and an Our Lady of Sorrows, placed at the outside extremes of the great arch dividing the choir from the church, in the semicircle of which, in eight compartments, eight half-length figures of prophets were painted. At the base of the arch was written in color MDLXVI . . . The destruction of these paintings, threatened for many years because of the rebuilding of the church, took place in 1813; but the writer has made drawings of the figures which he keeps for himself as very precious possessions."

1567. MARY MAGDALENE; ST PETER THE MARTYR; ST CATHERINE. From the correspondence between Titian, Giannantonio Facchinetti, Bishop of Nicastro, and Cardinal Farnese, it appears that in 1567–68 the artist had sent as a gift to Alessandro Farnese "a picture of St Mary Magdalene in the desert, in an attitude of devotion and repentance"; to Cardinal Michele di Bonelli a "St Catherine"; and to Pope Pius V a "Martyrdom of St Peter the Martyr." Gronau believes the *Mary Magdalene* is the one now in Capodimonte in Naples (plate 179) and the *St Catherine* in the painting now in the Museum of Fine Arts in Boston (plate 180); we have a reproduction of *St Peter the Martyr* in the engraving made by Bertelli and included here as plate 198.

1567. MADONNA. On May 3, 1567, Titian notified the Duke of Urbino that he had sent him "many, many days ago . . . by way of your Secretary, the picture of Our Lady" (Zanobi-Bicchierai, *Lettere d'illustri italiani per le nozze Galeotti-Cardenas*, Florence, 1864; Cavalcaselle).

1567. NUDE VENUS. On December 2, 1567, Titian notified Philip II that he would send him, together with *The Martyrdom of St Lawrence* (plate 121), a "nude Venus" painted by him after he had finished the canvas of the "Blessed Lawrence" (Simancas Archives, Cavalcaselle).

Before 1568. ALLEGORY OF RELIGION. It is apparent from the list of paintings on mythological subjects offered to Maximilian II by Titian that the artist had already sent the emperor a painting representing "religion" (cf. notes to plates 130 and 185, and, immediately below in this section under the year 1568, *Seven mythological "fables"*).

1568. SEVEN MYTHOLOGICAL "FABLES". "*Venit superioribus diebus ad me Titianus, ille pictor eximius, mihique dixit, quod iam antiquario caesareae maiestatis vestrae, cognominato Strada, fabulas praesertim nonnullas manu propria pictas ostendit, quae sibi vehementer placere visae sunt, ita ut dixerit, fabulas illas dignas quidem esse, ut in quodam palatio caesareae maiestatis vestrae reponerentur, ob idque unam ex illis praedicto antiquario reddidit sibi postea demonstrandam; quas quidem fabulas, ut ipse quoque videre vellem, instanter a me petiit in eoque sibi satisfacere coactus fui. Eas igitur vidi, quae profecto, ni fallor, tales sunt, ut in pisis nihil penitus desiderari posse videatur. Quae omnia ad dicti Titiani requisitionem significare et simul fabularum notam in istis inclusam caesareae maiestati vestrae transmittere necesse fuit. Datae Venetiis die 28. novembris 1568.*" "The fable of Endymion and Diana. The fable of Actaeon at the spring. The fable of the same, transformed into a stag and torn to pieces by his dogs. The fable of Callisto, discovered pregnant at the spring. The fable of Adonis, who went home against the wishes of Venus and was killed by the Wild Boar. The fable of Andromeda, bound to the rock and set free by Perseus. The fable of Europa, carried off by Jove transformed into a bull. And all the above-mentioned pictures are well on the way to being finished, and are a hands-breadth wider than that representing religion which has already been sent to your Imperial Majesty since it has more figures in it than the pictures depicting the fables have." Postscript to Veit von Dornberg's letter of November 28, 1568, to the Emperor Maximilian II. On December 8, the Emperor, replying to Von Dornberg's letter, showed himself to be most interested in the pictures Titian was offering him: *"Quod vero in appendice earundem literarum tuarum mentionem fecisti picturarum quarundam, quas antiquus et excellens ille Titianus pictor confecit et quas antiquarius quoque noster Jacobus Strada tantopere commendavit, ut dignas iudicavit quae in palatio aliquo nostro collocentur, volumus, ut, cum omnes illae picturae fabularum, quarum indicem nobis misisti, fuerint absolutae, cognoscas ex ipso pictore Titiano, quanti easdem aestimet et num artifitio respondeant iis picturis, quas ille fecit antehac, dum esset iunior et visu magis vigeret. Veremur enim, cum senes sensu et presertim visu deficere soleant, ut sibimet in conficiendis ingeniosis picturis adhuc similis existat, sed dubitamus, eum non amplius in arte sua prestare sicut olim, dum esset ingenii et maturis viribus integer. Itaque de his abs te certum responsum et plenam informationen expectabimus. Datum in oppido nostro Lintz die 8. decembris 1568."* On December 26, Von Dornberg assured Maximilian that he would obey his wishes and would send him the information requested as soon as he had obtained it (*Jahrbuch der Kunsthistorische Sammlungen,* XIII/II, Reg. 8804, 8806, 8808). Cf. notes to plates 130 and 185.

c. 1570. TARQUIN AND LUCRETIA, *canvas, 187 × 127.* Mentioned by Anonimo del Tizianello (1622) as belonging to the Earl of Arundel, who offered it to Charles I of England; it is noted in Charles's collection by Ridolfi (1648). In 1649 it became the property of Cardinal Mazarin and then of Louis XIV (1661). Already noted as "endommagé et à rentoiler" in 1752 by Leipicié (*Catalogue raisonné des tableaux du roi,* 1754, No. 31), in 1802 it came to the Musée de Bordeaux, and was heavily damaged in the 1870 fire (F. Ingersoll-Smouse, 1926). Now it has disappeared (Tietze, 1950). According to Ingersoll-Smouse, it might have been a first version of the picture in the Fitzwilliam Museum in Cambridge (plate 136).

Before 1574. VENUS'S TOILETTE. In the list of paintings executed for Philip II and not yet paid for, which Titian included in his letter sent on December 22, 1754, to the King of Spain (Simancas Archives, Secretariat of State, Leg. 1336), a "Venus with Cupid who is holding her mirror" is mentioned (cf. note to plate 62). It is probably that described by Argote da Molina in 1582. Two pictures on this subject are mentioned as still being in Spain in the Royal Collections in the eighteenth century (C. Justi, 1889).

1574. NATIVITY. On December 22, 1574, Titian wrote to Philip II that he should expect a "manger scene" (Simancas Archives, Secretariat of State, Leg. 1336).

1575. ST JEROME. Mentioned by Guzman de Silva as being among the pictures sent to Philip II on September 24, 1575 (Beroqui, 1946).

UNDATED PAINTINGS

PORTRAIT OF FRANCESCO AS-
SONICA; REST ON THE FLIGHT
INTO EGYPT. "In the house of
Messer Francesco Sonica the lawyer
and a friend of Titian, is the portrait
of this same Messer Francesco by
Titian, and in a big picture Our
Lady, who, on her way into Egypt,
has got down from the donkey and is
sitting on a rock by the roadside.
St Joseph is by the side of the young
St John who is giving the Christ
Child some flowers picked by an
Angel from the boughs of a tree
which is in the middle of the wooded
landscape full of animals; in the
distance the ass can be seen grazing.
This picture, which is most beautiful,
has been put by the above-mentioned
gentleman in one of his houses, the
one he has built in Padua near Santa
Iustina" (Vasari). A record of the
big picture, mentioned by Ridolfi as
being in Venice, remains in a 1569
engraving by M. Rota, while in
another engraving by Cochin it is
noted that the picture itself was lost
with the galley which was carrying it
to Spain. Some scholars have identified it with the picture in the Prado
given in 1644 to Philip IV (Tietze).
The portrait of Assonica is also mentioned by Ridolfi as being in Venice,
in the house of Pietro Assonica.

PORTRAIT OF GIOVANNI VAN
HAANEN; MADONNA AND CHILD
AND PORTRAITS OF MEMBERS OF
THE VAN HAANEN HOUSEHOLD.
Vasari mentions as being in Giovanni
van Haanen's house in Venice (apart
from the *Ecce Homo* today in the

Vienna Kunsthistorisches Museum—
Part 2, plate 174), the portrait of the
head of the family "which seems
alive," and "a picture of Our Lady
with other figures, very life-like—
human beings and cherubs all drawn
from life and from people in that
house." The picture is noted by
Sansovino again in 1581 in the Van
Haanen house at San Benedetto.
Vasari's placing of these three pictures among the youthful works of
Titian makes an early dating seem
likely; this, however, is contradicted
by the definite date of 1543 for the
Ecce Homo.

CHRIST CARRYING THE CROSS.
Mentioned by Sansovino (1581) as
being in the Chapel of Federico
Vallareso in Sant'Andrea della Cer-
tosa in Venice.

ST JEROME. In the house of Pietro
Servio, in Venice, "a St Jerome of
Messer Titian" (M. Michiel, hand-
written note after 1575).

BIRTH OF JESUS. Burned in January
1578 when it was displayed on the
main altar of San Marco (Cicogna,
1653, VI/2nd).

PORTRAIT OF KING LUDOVIC OF
HUNGARY. Listed as No. 1216 in the
1598–1607 inventory of Palazzo
Reale in Madrid (R. Beer, 1898).

PORTRAIT OF JUAN ALBIN, THE
ENGLISH PAINTER. Listed as the
previous painting (C. Justi, 1889;
R. Beer, 1898; A. L. Mayer, 1938;
possibly a portrait of Hans Holbein).

PORTRAIT OF CARDINAL ACCOLTI OF RAVENNA. Noted by Vasari in the "dressing-room" of Duke Cosimo in Florence.

PORTRAIT OF ERCOLE II, DUKE OF FERRARA. Mentioned by Vasari in the life of Girolamo da Carpi.

PORTRAIT OF FRANCESCO FILETTO AND HIS SON. "He painted the portrait of Messer Francesco Filetto, the orator of happy memory, and in the same picture, in front of him, one of his sons, who seemed alive; this portrait is in the house of Messer Matteo Giustiniano, the art lover" (Vasari). The identification of this picture with the two portraits in the Vienna Kunsthistorisches Museum (plates 8 and 9) has been shown to be untenable.

PORTRAIT OF CARDINAL GONZAGA, BROTHER OF THE DUKE OF MANTUA. Mentioned by Vasari.

PORTRAIT OF CARDINAL DOMENICO GRIMANI. Recorded in the sixteenth century in the Grimani house at Santa Maria Formosa (Cicogna, 1853, I/190).

PORTRAIT OF GIOVANNI FRACASTORO. Mentioned by Vasari. Its identification with the portrait in the Museo Civico di Castelvecchio in Verona (Part 2, plate 223) is not convincing.

PORTRAIT OF THE DOGE LEONARDO LOREDAN. Mentioned by Vasari.

TWO FEMALE PORTRAITS: the "Rossa, wife of the Great Turk at the age of sixteen, and Cameria, her daughter, both with beautiful clothes and headdresses." Mentioned by Vasari (G. Gronau, 1903).

PORTRAIT OF MASSIMIANO STAMPA, Commander of the Castello in Milan. Mentioned by Vasari.

PORTRAIT OF NICCOLO ZENO. Mentioned by Vasari and also by Ridolfi.

PORTRAIT OF A GENTLEWOMAN. "In the house of a gentleman of the Pisani family near San Marco, the portrait of a gentlewoman is by Titian and is a marvelous work" (Vasari).

PORTRAIT OF A GENTLEMAN. "And our sculptor Danese has in his house in Venice a portrait, by Titian, of a gentleman of the Dolfini family" (Vasari).

PAINTINGS ATTRIBUTED
TO TITIAN

Plate 147a
PORTRAIT OF POPE PAUL III.
Canvas, 98 × 79. Leningrad, Hermitage.
Acquired in 1850 from the Barbarigo
family. Cavalcaselle and Ricketts are
uncertain as to the painter; L.
Venturi (1912) considers the painting
to be a mediocre copy; Suida and
Tietze believe it to be a genuine
Titian; Tietze-Conrat (1946) thinks
it is the "model" for the 1543 portrait
kept by Titian in his workshop and
sold to the Barbarigo family by
Pomponio. Pallucchini does not
agree with Tietze-Conrat's theory,
and believes the painting to be
derived from that of Paul III "with
the papal cap" in Capodimonte in
Naples, given here as plate 2, Part 3.

Plate 147b
PORTRAIT OF POPE PAUL III.
*Canvas, 89 × 78. Vienna, Kunsthis-
torisches Museum.* Mostly thought,
with reason, to be by Titian's school;
however, Berenson (1957) catalogs
it as mostly by Titian himself.

Plate 148a
PORTRAIT OF POPE JULIUS II.
Panel, 99 × 82. Florence, Pitti Palace.
May possibly be identifiable with the
portrait, by Titian, of this pope
seen by Vasari in the "dressing-
room" of the Duke of Urbino, who
had commissioned it in 1546. It
came to Florence in 1631, and in the
inventory taken that year is listed as a
Raphael; however, in the inventories of 1691 and 1694 of Palazzo

Pitti it is ascribed to Titian. Cavalcaselle thinks in terms of Giovanni da
Udine; Burckhardt of a Venetian
artist; A. Venturi first in terms of
one of Titian's followers, then of
Raphael (1926), and then believed
the painting to be later than the great
Urbino master. Gronau believes it
was painted in Titian's workshop
and under his guidance; Tietze omits
it from his catalog and remarks on
it as being in the Venetian style in his
note on the Uffizi *Portrait of Sixtus
IV* (cf. note on p. 126, Part 1).
Berenson, Ortolani (1948), Pallucchini and Dell'Acqua (1955) all
believe it to be an authentic Titian,
based on the lost original by Raphael
in the Church of Santa Maria del
Popolo.

Plate 148b
PORTRAIT OF CARDINAL ALES-
SANDRO FARNESE. *Panel, 51 × 48.
Tivoli, Villa d'Este.* Early attributed
to Raphael, and engraved under his
name by De Rossi in 1730. Cavalcaselle, Gronau, Tietze and Pallucchini attribute it to Titian (the latter
critic dates it to about 1545–46);
di Carpegna considers it definitely to
be by a Mannerist painter, possibly
Pierin del Vaga (*Catalogo della
Quadreria di Villa d'Este a Tivoli,*
n.d.).

Plate 149
SUPPOSED PORTRAIT OF VITTORIA
FARNESE. *Panel, 80 × 61.5. Buda-
pest, Museum of Fine Arts.* From

Count Janos Palffy's Collection. Ascribed to Titian by Berenson (1926) and Gombosi (1928), who, on the basis of a coat-of-arms of the Farnese family on the reverse of the painting, identifies it with that described in 1680 in Palazzo del Giardino in Parma (Campori), which according to this scholar is a portrait of Vittoria Farnese, daughter of Pier Luigi and wife (in 1547) of Guidobaldo II, Duke of Urbino, painted in Rome in 1546. The identification and the Titian attribution are both accepted by Fogolari (1935) and Berenson (1957), while Suida ascribes the painting to Salviati. Mayer, followed by Pallucchini, thinks quite rightly that it is a copy of a Titian painting executed by an artist in Parmigianino's circle; for Tietze, not only is it not a Venetian painting, but he does not believe that it has anything to do with Titian at all.

SUPPOSED PORTRAIT OF GIULIA VARANA. *Panel, 111.8 × 85.1. Florence, Pitti Palace.* Gronau (1936) identifies this picture as the portrait of Giulia Varana, wife of Guidobaldo II, Duke of Urbino, which Pietro Aretino mentioned in a letter in October 1545, and which is also mentioned in the Urbino correspondence for the years 1546-47. Mayer (1938) believes it to be an authentic Titian; Berenson (1957) believes much of it to be by Titian himself; Wilde (1930), followed by Tietze and Pallucchini, judges it to be a copy (by Rubens?) of a lost Titian original (cf. Lost Paintings, 1545-46, *Portrait of Giulia Varana*, etc.). Reproduced in H. Tietze, *Titien*, 1950, French edition, Fig. 308.

Plate 150
PORTRAIT OF A MAN IN FURS. *Canvas, 94 × 70. São Paulo, Museu d'Arte.* Formerly in the collections of Abraham Hume; Lord Alfred Hume; Lord Brownlow in Belton House, Grantham (Lincolnshire); Wildenstein in New York. The picture, which, it has been suggested, represents a member of the Contarini family, is accepted as an authentic Titian by, among others, Suida, L. Venturi (1933), and Berenson, who proposes dating it 1545-46. Tietze does not accept the Titian attribution.

Plate 151
THE EDUCATION OF LOVE. *Canvas, 180 × 115. New York, Kress Collection.* Suida (1952) identifies it with the painting listed in the 1621 inventory of Rudolf II's collection (H. Zimmermann, 1905), which was taken to Prague in 1648 by Swedish troops and transferred to the collection of Queen Christina of Sweden, and then transferred with the collection to Rome, going later to the gallery of the Duke of Orléans. When this collection was broken up during the French Revolution, the painting was bought by Earl Gower, Marquis of Stafford, first Duke of Sutherland; until 1930 it remained in the Stafford House Collection, then going to the A. L. Nicolson Collection in London. Cavalcaselle thinks it is probably by Schiavone. Suida believes it to be a genuine Titian dating from about 1546, and has reaffirmed his belief in this attribution after the picture's recent restoration (1952), citing the favorable opinions of Gronau, Von Hadeln, Mayer and A. Venturi, and pointing out how the idea for the composition came from Correggio's painting executed for Federico Gonzaga which is now in the National Gallery in London. Pallucchini accepts the Titian attribution; Tietze and Berenson (1957) do not.

Plate 152

DANAË. *Canvas, 121 × 170. New York, Hickox Collection.* Formerly in the collections of the Earl of Chesterfield and of Annesley Gore. A replica from Titian's workshop, with variations, of the painting in the Gallerie Nazionali of Naples (plates 4–5), it is believed to be an authentic Titian by Von Hadeln (1926) and Berenson (1957).

Plate 153a

PORTRAIT OF THE DOGE FRANCESCO DONATO. *Canvas, 99.9 × 79. San Diego, Fine Arts Gallery.* Formerly in the collections of Lord Battersea and Anthony Rothschild in London, it came to the Gallery in 1941 (Catalogue of the Gallery, 1947). Published as an authentic Titian by Suida (1946) and Tietze-Conrat (1947), independently of each other. Tietze believes it to be Titian's prototype for the official portrait of this Doge painted between 1545 and 1553 (cf. Lost Paintings, *Portrait of the Doge Francesco Donato*). Mayer attributes it to Tintoretto. It is quite rightly deleted from Berenson's catalogue of Titian's works (1957).

Plate 153b

PORTRAIT OF A MAN WITH GLOVES. *Canvas, 98.3 × 74.2. Munich, Bohler Collection.* Came from an old Genoese collection. Von Hadeln recognized it as a genuine Titian, and Martini published it as such (1957), suggesting a date of 1545–50.

Plate 154a

DOUBLE PORTRAIT. *Canvas, 123 × 96. Padua, private collection.* Bears the inscription: T.V.F., with the date: MDLII underneath; also, at the top on the right: ANNO AETATIS XXX, and at the bottom on the left: AETATIS S. VIII. Bologna published it as an authentic Titian (1957); however, it is difficult to make a definite judgment on account of the deterioration of the original paint.

Plate 154b

PORTRAIT OF A VENETIAN NOBLEMAN. *Canvas, 121 × 93. New York, Metropolitan Museum, Bache Collection.* Formerly in the collections of Alberto Giovanelli in Venice, and Duveen in New York. Mayer considers it to be an authentic Titian (1930), as do L. Venturi (1931), who dates it to about 1522; Suida; and Berenson (1957), who believes it was painted after 1555. Tietze does not mention it.

Plate 155a

SUPPOSED PORTRAIT OF FERDINAND I. *Canvas, 99 × 74. Naples, Capodimonte.* It was originally in Palazzo Farnese in Rome, and was transferred in 1662 to Parma, where it is listed in the 1680 inventory of Palazzo del Giardino. Cavalcaselle, who is doubtful of its authenticity as a Titian, identifies it with the portrait of Emperor Charles V which Titian sent in 1549 to Ferrante Gonzaga, the governor of Milan; this identification is accepted by De Rinaldis (1928, *Catalogo della Galleria*), Fogolari (1935), and Berenson (cf. Lost Paintings, 1549, *Portrait of Charles V*). However, Fischel's suggestion is more convincing: taking into consideration the age of the sitter, he thinks that the picture portrays Ferdinand, younger brother of Charles V. Pallucchini, while tending to accept Fischel's hypothesis, rightly judges the picture to have been painted by Titian's workshop; Tietze, following Dussler (1935), believes that the portrait is probably an authentic Titian—although he is not certain as to whether it is a copy or an original.

85

Plate 155b

PORTRAIT OF ANDREA DE' FRAN-
CESCHI. *Canvas, 86.5 × 68.5.
Indianapolis, Collection of G. H. A.
Clowes.* This is a third portrait of
Andrea de' Franceschi, Great Chancellor of the City of Venice from
1529 to 1532—a later one, judging by
the sitter's age, than those in the
National Gallery in Washington and
the Detroit Museum (part III, plates
214a and b). Suida (1956) believes
that it may be the portrait mentioned
by Ridolfi in the De' Franceschi
family's house. Berenson is uncertain
as to whether the picture is an
authentic Titian or not (1957).

Plate 156a

SUPPOSED PORTRAIT OF ANDREA
VESALIO. *Canvas, 128 × 98. Florence, Pitti Palace.* Came from the
estate of Prince Ferdinando de'
Medici. Cavalcaselle had already
judged it indecipherable, and rightly
so, because of heavy repainting; he
also notes that by comparison with
the portrait of Vesalio engraved by
Calcar, the traditional identification
of this picture is anything but convincing. Suida and Berenson believe
it to be an authentic Titian; Gronau
and Tietze omit it from the catalog
of authenticated works by the master.

Plate 156b

PORTRAIT OF PHILIP II. *Canvas,
108 × 78. Rome, Barberini Palace.*
Formerly in the Corsini Collection.
Traditionally attributed to Titian,
but generally considered by contemporary critics to be a replica from
Titian's workshop of a lost original
—which must have differed icono-
graphically from the portraits in the
Prado in Madrid and in Capodimonte in Naples (plates 43 and 48),
and derived, according to Gombosi
(1928–29), from the Fleming-French
prototype at Hampton Court.

Among the other paintings of this
type portraying Philip II, that in the
Prado is attributed to Sanchéz Coello
by Mayer (1925) and the one in
Palazzo Rosso in Genoa to Van
Dyck (N. di Carpegna, 1953).

PORTRAIT OF PHILIP II. *Canvas,
185 × 91. Pitti Palace.* Vasari saw a
portrait of Philip II in the "dressing-
room" of Grand Duke Cosimo I.
Berenson and Gronau both consider
it to be a genuine Titian, and the
latter critic thinks that it was painted
in Milan in 1548, or in Augsburg in
1550; Tietze and Pallucchini main-
tain that it is a version dating
from the same time as the Naples
portrait (plate 48, Part 3), as Cavalcaselle had already suggested. Reproduced in *Münchner Jahrbuch*, 1925,
p. 270.

SELF-PORTRAIT. *Canvas, diameter
107.* Formerly in Berlin in the R. von
Kaufmann Collection. According to
Gronau (1936–37), it may probably
be identified with the self-portrait
listed in the 1567–69 inventory of
Gabriele Vendramin's Collection (A.
Ravà, 1920), and mentioned by
Pietro Aretino in a sonnet following
a letter of his written in July 1550—
V/518 (cf. Lost Paintings, 1550).
Quite rightly, art critics have not
accepted this attribution. Reproduced in *Bollettino d'Arte*, 1936–37,
p. 291.

Plate 157

PORTRAIT OF THE DUKE OF
ACQUAVIVA. *Canvas, 140 × 102.
Lucerne, Collection of Julius Bohler.*
Bears the inscription: GIOVANNI
ACQUAVIVA . . . ATRI ANNO MDLI
and the signature: TITANVS F. Came
from a Polish collection. Von Hadeln
(1934) was the first to suggest that
this portrait of Giovanni Francesco,
Duke of Acquaviva and Duke of

Atri, is an authentic Titian—a proposal which has, quite rightly, been rejected by Tietze and by Berenson.

Plate 158

CHRIST BETWEEN TWO EXECUTIONERS. *Panel, diameter 117. Paris, Louvre.* Formerly in the collection of Louis XIV. Cavalcaselle considers it to be "in the style of" Schiavone; Gronau believes it is an authentic Titian, and tends to identify it with the "Christ with two figures, one on either side, by Messer Titian, complete with circular frame" listed in the 1567–69 inventory of the Vendramin Collection (A. Ravà, 1920); Suida, quite properly, judges it to be a copy; while Berenson thinks it is a fragment of a larger composition mostly painted by Titian's workshop.

Plate 159

TRIPTYCH. *Castello Roganzuolo (Ceneda), Parish Church.* In the center, the *Madonna and Child*, canvas, 240 × 80; on the left, *St Paul*, canvas, 190 × 57; on the right, *St Peter*, canvas, 190 × 57. It was placed in the church in 1549, and the payments for it, begun in 1543, were prolonged until 1560. According to Cavalcaselle, the original triptych was replaced in 1575 by a standard of Orazio Vecellio. Gronau, among others, believes the triptych is an authentic Titian, and agrees in rejecting Cavalcaselle's hypothesis (A. Gardin, 1883). In spite of the damage it suffered during the First World War (Moschetti, 1952), it must certainly be considered as a work painted by Titian's workshop on an idea of Titian's—as Pallucchini has also recently observed.

Plate 160

POLYPTYCH. *Dubrovnik, Cathedral.* In the center: *The Assumption*, canvas, 344 × 172; on the left, *SS Lazzaro and Biagio*, canvas, 200 × 55; on the right: *SS Nicholas of Bari and Anthony Abbot*, canvas, 200 × 55; above: *The Angel of the Annunciation*, canvas, 100 × 55, and *The Virgin of the Annunciation*, canvas, 100 × 55 (the two latter compartments are not reproduced here). Originally in the Church of San Lazzaro Outside-the-Walls. Gamulin (1955 and 1956) quite rightly considers this polyptych to have been painted by Titian's workshop in the fifth decade of the sixteenth century, with the help of Francesco Vecellio and Titian himself, and judges it to be close to the Castello Roganzuolo *Triptych* (plate 159), and slightly earlier than the Lentiai polyptych (plate 36).

Plate 161a

MARY MAGDALENE, WITH ST BIAGIO, TOBIAS, THE ANGEL, AND THE DONOR. *Canvas, 208 × 163. Dubrovnik, Church of St Dominic.* Cavalcaselle has already considered it to be from Titian's workshop with the participation of Titian himself, while Berenson believes this participation to be of major importance. Pallucchini and Gamulin (1957) do not exclude such an intervention, and date the picture to the fifth decade, between the Castello Roganzuolo *Triptytch* (plate 159) and the Lentiai polyptych (plate 36).

THE HOLY FAMILY WORSHIPPED BY THE DONOR AND HIS HOUSEHOLD. *Canvas, 118 × 161. Dresden, Gemäldegalerie.* In the seventeenth century it was taken from Ferrara to the Ducal Collection in Modena, and from there to the Gallery in 1746. Listed as a work by Titian in the Modena and Dresden inventories, after which Cavalcaselle attributed it to Titian's school (Marco or Orazio Vecellio), and Wickhoff (1913) to Antonio Badile. Today it is generally considered to have been painted by Titian's workshop. Berenson (1957) still believes that the figure of the Madonna was painted by Titian himself after 1555. Reproduced in *Klassiker der Kunst, Tizian*, 1906, p. 166.

Plate 161b

CRUCIFIXION. *Panel, 23.3 × 17. Madrid, Royal Palace.* Listed in the 1574 Escorial inventory, in which particular mention is made of the small panel with the figure of St John the Baptist which closed the case containing the small Crucifixion (C. Justi, 1889; I. Milicua, 1957). Fiocco (1956) identifies this painting with the one Titian, in a letter dated September 29, 1559, presented to Philip II as a gift from his son Orazio. Fiocco and Berenson believe it to be an authentic Titian; Braunfels (1957), on the other hand, considers it the work of Orazio Vecellio. However, this small panel is definitely of a better quality than any of the known works of Orazio, as Fiocco quite rightly observes (1959). This leads to the supposition that Titian himself did it.

Plate 162a

JOVE AND ANTIOPE. *Canvas on panel, 61 × 51. Munich, Bayerische Staatsgemäldesammlungen.* Formerly in the Electoral Gallery in Munich. Probably a fragment of a much larger painting. Listed in the early catalogs as a work by Paolo Veronese, but attributed to Titian in the eighteenth-century inventories. Cavalcaselle ascribes it to Giovanni Contarini; Suida and A. Venturi (1927) return to the Titian attribution, this latter critic suggesting a date of about 1554 for its execution;

neither Tietze nor Berenson accepts it as an authentic Titian.

Plate 162b

VENUS AND ADONIS. *Canvas, 187 × 184. Rome, Barberini Palace.* Formerly in the collection of Queen Christina of Sweden in Palazzo Riario alla Lungara in Rome (Campori, 1870). Acquired in 1689 by Cardinal Azzolini, then by the Odescalchi family, and finally by the Torlonia family. It is one of the best of the many replicas painted by Titian's workshop of the famous Prado painting (plate 57). A. Venturi (1896) considers it to be an old derivation from the London painting (plate 56); Di Carpegna (1953) believes it to be a replica painted by Titian himself, although with extensive help from his workshop (*Catalogo della Galleria Nazionale, Palazzo Barberini*, Rome, 1953).

Plate 163a

NYMPH AND FAUN. *Canvas, 63 × 53.5. Rotterdam, Boymans Museum.* Perhaps originally in the Barbarigo Collection; Boymans bequest 1847. Tietze believes it may be the painting representing "Siringa being raped by Pan . . ." mentioned by Ridolfi as being in Titian's house until his death. Schmidt-Degener attributes it to Dosso Dossi (in *The Burlington Magazine*, 1916), while Suida returns to the Titian attribution (French edition), followed by Tietze (1939)—who suggests about 1560—and Tietze-Conrat (1955). Berenson does not include it in his catalogue of Titian's paintings (1957).

Plate 163b

PORTRAIT OF A MAN WITH BOOK. *Canvas, 107.5 × 84. Copenhagen, Statens Museum for Kunst.* Formerly in the West and Spengler (1809) collections as a work by Titian. Madsen (in *Kunstbladet*, 1898) identified it—without foundation—as the portrait of Francesco Maria della Rovere; Höyen attributes it to Paris Bordone. The 1951 *Catalogue of the Museum* attributes it to Titian, as does Pallucchini, who dates it to the early 1560s. Neither Tietze nor Berenson mention it in their Titian catalogs.

Plate 164a

SUPPOSED PORTRAIT OF FILIPPO STROZZI. *Canvas, 117 × 90. Vienna, Kunsthistorisches Museum.* Listed in the collection of the Archduke Leopold Wilhelm in 1659. The identification of the sitter with Filippo Strozzi—a sworn enemy of the Medici family who died in 1538—which was first suggested in the *Catalogue of the Belvedere* in 1783, seems contradicted by the late style of the painting. Suida and Tietze date it about 1540, Mayer (1924) to a decade later. Baldass and Gronau reject the Titian attribution.

Plate 164b

PORTRAIT OF A BEARDED MAN. *Canvas, 113.5 × 93.5. Copenhagen, Statens Museum for Kunst.* Acquired in 1926 and published by Madsen in the same year in *Samleren*, it is considered by most critics to be an authentic Titian dating from the sixth decade, and was exhibited as such at the Titian Exhibition in Venice (Fogolari, 1935). Tietze removes it from his catalog of the master's paintings.

VENUS BLINDFOLDING CUPID. *Canvas, 96 × 66. Milan, private collection.* Fiocco (1957) considers it to be an authentic Titian and identifies it with the painting of which Van Dyck made a sketch which is probably in the Arundel Collection in England (O. Fischel, in *Old Master Drawings*, 1933). Reproduced in *Arte Veneta*, 1957, p. 203.

PORTRAIT OF A GENTLEWOMAN WITH VASE. *Canvas, 99.5 × 88. Dresden, Gemäldegalerie.* Came in 1746 from the Ducal Collections in Modena. Morelli believes it was painted by Titian, and so does Berenson (1957), dating it after 1555. Most contemporary critics quite rightly reject the Titian attribution, including Cavalcaselle (B. Licinio) and Wickhoff (1913: a Florentine painter). Reproduced in Suida, *Tiziano*, Fig. CLXXXIX.

SUPPOSED PORTRAIT OF LAVINIA. *Canvas, 111.5 × 90. Vienna, Kunsthistorisches Museum.* Formerly in the Collection of the Archduke Leopold Wilhelm, where it is listed in the 1659 inventory as a work by Titian. The sitter is identified as Titian's daughter on the basis of a slight resemblance to the Dresden painting (plate 97). Von Hadeln (1931), Suida and Berenson (1957) believe it to be an authentic Titian; Stix (in *Jahrbuch der Kunsthistorische Sammlungen*, XXXI, 1914), Ozzola (1931: Marco Vecellio?), Tietze and Pallucchini, on the other hand, quite rightly believe it was painted by Titian's workshop. Reproduced in Suida, *Tiziano*, Fig. CCIV.

Plate 165

PORTRAIT OF A NOBLEWOMAN. *Canvas, 98 × 74. Washington, National Gallery of Art, Kress Collection, 1939.* Formerly in the Wilbraham Collection, Delamere House, England; in the Kress Collection from 1939 onwards. The portrait, which has been variously identified as being of Giulia Gonzaga Colonna or of Titian's daughter Lavinia, is considered to be an authentic Titian by Suida, Berenson and Pallucchini, who suggests a date of about 1550-55. Tietze, however, does not include it in his Titian catalog.

Plate 166

PORTRAIT OF THE DOGE MAR-CANTONIO TREVISAN. *Canvas, 103 × 86.5. Budapest, Museum of Fine Arts*. From the collection of Janos Palffy. The Titian attribution is accepted by Suida and Berenson, but quite rightly doubted by Von Hadeln (1931) and Tietze, among others.

Plate 167a

PORTRAIT OF A MONK. *Canvas, 66 × 57. Bowood (Calne, Wilts), Collection of the Marquis of Lansdowne*. Exhibited (No. 36) in the "Loan Exhibition of forty-nine Master-pieces of Venetian Painting" at Agnew's in London, 1953. It is certainly a fragment of a larger painting, and is considered to be an authentic Titian by Pallucchini (1953), who dates it to between 1550 and 1560, and by Berenson (1957).

Plate 167b

ECCE HOMO. *Canvas, 74.9 × 59.7. Dublin, National Gallery of Ireland*. Listed as a work by Titian in Christie's sale on May 21, 1885. The 1914 *Catalogue of the Gallery* attributed it to Matteo Cerezo. J. Gore (1955) has returned to the Titian attribution, suggesting a date of about 1560, followed by Berenson (1957).

Plate 168

CHRIST AND SIMON OF CYRENE. *Canvas, 98 × 116. Madrid, Prado*. Bears the inscription: I. B. TITIANVS. The initials "I.B." were in the past mistakenly believed to be those of Giovanni Bellini. Listed for the first time in 1574 in Philip II's Oratory in the Escorial as a work by Titian. This attribution is upheld by Caval-caselle, Fischel (who dates it 1560), Ricketts (who believes it was probably begun in 1540–50 and finished in about 1560), Suida and Berenson (who sees in it the inter-vention of Titian's workshop). The Titian attribution is rejected by Wickhoff (1904: Palma Giovane), Tietze (a Spanish imitator of Titian) and Pallucchini, who quite rightly believes the canvas to have been painted by Titian's workshop.

Plate 169

ECCE HOMO. *Canvas, 50 × 64. Escorial, Monastery of St Lawrence*. Mentioned for the first time by Ponz (1773) as a work by Titian, it was later ascribed to Tintoretto. R. Longhi (1954) returns to the Titian attribution with a date of about 1560. Berenson (1957) omits it from his Titian catalog. Restora-tion may bring to light details characteristic of the work of Titian himself which already seem highly probable.

MATER DOLOROSA. *Canvas, 84 × 68.5. Madrid, Museo Cerralbo*. According to an inscription on the reverse, this painting comes from the collection of Prince Fondi in Naples. Mayer (1937) believes it to be a replica by Titian himself, painted after 1560, of the Prado *Our Lady of Sorrows* (plate 55). Neither Tietze nor Berenson include it in their Titian catalogs. Reproduced in *L'Arte*, 1935, p. 375.

ST JOHN THE BAPTIST. *Canvas, 185 × 110. Escorial, Monastery of St Lawrence*. Signed: TITIANVS FAC . . . . Cavalcaselle, Suida (1927) and Mayer (1957) consider it to be a later version—dating from about 1560—of the painting in the Acca-demia in Venice (Part 2, plate 172). The Titian attribution is not ac-cepted by either Tietze or Berenson (1957). Reproduced in *The Burlington Magazine*, 1937, p. 176, Fig. E.

ALLEGORICAL SCENE. *Canvas, 129.9 × 155.3. Chicago, Art Institute.* Formerly in the collections of the Earl of Wemyss, Gosford House; Wildenstein, Paris and New York; Thyssen, Munich; Ch. and M. Worcester, Chicago. Valentiner (1930) and L. Venturi (1932) accept the Titian attribution; it is quite rightly rejected by most critics, following Cavalcaselle. Panofsky and Tietze-Conrat (1945) believe it is an inverted copy of a lost original (see also Adriani, 1941). The artist might be Domenico Mazza, since a similar painting—in Palazzo Donà in Venice —is attributed to him by Ridolfi (Tietze). Pallucchini does not agree with this identification, ascribing the painting to an unknown pupil of Titian's. Berenson believes the canvas was partly painted by Titian himself. Reproduced in *L'Arte*, 1932, p. 491.

PORTRAIT OF IRENE DI SPILIM-BERGO. *Canvas, 122 × 106.5. Washington, National Gallery, Widener Collection.* Bears the inscription: SI FATA TULISSENT. Formerly in the possession of the Spilimbergo family and then in the Collection of Count Fabio Maniago. This painting and the following canvas portraying Emilia di Spilimbergo were traditionally attributed—largely because of a mistaken interpretation on Vasari's part—to Titian (F. Maniago, 1823), and were reproduced with this attribution in the 1942 *Catalogue of the National Gallery*, as well as being included by Berenson in his Titian catalog of 1957. Today, however, they are generally considered to be works by Giovanni Paolo Pase—mainly because the documents (which have disappeared) attesting to Titian's work seemed to have been tampered with (M. Muraro,

1949). H. Tietze and Tietze-Conrat (1953), in carrying out a definitive survey of the question, consider the landscape to the right of the figure of Irene "not unworthy of Titian's brush". Reproduced in *Emporium*, March 1953, p. 101.

PORTRAIT OF EMILIA DI SPILIM-BERGO. *Canvas, 122 × 106. Washington, National Gallery, Widener Collection.* See note to preceding painting. Reproduced in *Emporium*, March 1953, p. 98.

Plate 170
THE ADORATION OF THE MAGI. *Canvas, 110 × 132. Aarburg, W. Löthy Collection.* According to Tietze-Conrat (1934), the painting Titian executed for Cardinal Ippolito d'Este of Ferrara may be identified with this Aarburg painting rather than with the Ambrosiana version (plate 77). However, the picture's style would seem to exclude any participation by Titian himself.

Plate 171
THE ADORATION OF THE MAGI. *Canvas, 112 × 213. Cleveland, Museum of Art, W. H. Marlatt Collection.* Formerly in the following English collections: Welsch-Porter, sold in 1826; S. Rogers; Munzo; Butler Johnstone; Brocklebank, sold in 1922. Then in the Durlacher and Sachs collections in New York. Mayer at first believed this to be the painting sent to Spain in 1560, and later (1938) the best of the several versions of this painting, which is to be identified with the Escorial picture (plate 76). Berenson and Venturi (1931) consider this Cleveland painting to be an authentic Titian, and this latter citic, followed by Pallucchini, notes its late style. Tietze holds it to be a Spanish copy.

Plate 172

THE ADORATION OF THE MAGI. *Canvas, 141 × 219. Madrid, Prado.* Acquired by Charles IV, it appears in the 1818 Aranjuez inventory (Beroqui, 1946). Cavalcaselle believes it to be the painting sent to Philip II in 1560 (cf. note to plate 76); Morelli attributes it to Polidoro Lanzani; Mayer (1938) thinks it may have been painted by Luca Giordano. A. Venturi accepts the Titian attribution, which is rejected by Tietze, Pallucchini (who holds it to be a later replica), and in 1957 also by Berenson, who lists it as a painting by Titian's workshop.

ADORATION OF THE MAGI. *Canvas, 217 × 149. Paris, Atri Collection.* Made known by Mayer (1938), who considers this was the last version, begun by Titian and finished by his pupils, of this often-repeated subject (cf. notes to plates 76 and 77). Neither Berenson (1957) nor Tietze mentions the painting in their lists. Reproduced in *The Burlington Magazine*, 1937, p. 179, Fig. B.

Plate 173

MADONNA AND CHILD. *Canvas, 122.5 × 94. Rome, Albertini Collection.* Formerly in the collection of the Marquises of Mazenta, whose inventory (dated December 30, 1678) lists the painting as a work by Titian, after G. B. Crespi (called Cerano) had already attributed it to this master in 1628. It was acquired in Bergamo in 1916 by descendants of the Mazenta family (E. Modogliano, *La collectione di Luigi Albertini*, Rome, 1942). Suida and Berenson consider it to be a late work of Titian's, and it was exhibited as such at the 1930 London exhibition; Tietze omits it from his Titian catalogue; Longhi (1946) tends to consider it as the work of Jacopo Bassano.

Plate 174

PORTRAIT OF ARCHBISHOP FILIPPO ARCHINTO. *Canvas, 118.1 × 94. New York, Metropolitan Museum.* Formerly in the Archinto Collection in Milan, and the Altman Collection in New York, coming to the Museum in 1931 with the legacy of the latter. S. Monod's attribution (1923) of the painting to Titian about 1543-46 is accepted by Suida, Fischel and Berenson—who, however, date the portrait 1554-56, the years in which Archinto, Archbishop of Milan, was in exile in Venice. Tietze omits it from his catalogue of Titian's works; Pallucchini considers it to be largely painted by Titian's workshop, possibly on a sketch by the master himself.

PORTRAIT OF ARCHBISHOP FILIPPO ARCHINTO. *Canvas, 111 × 88. Philadelphia, Johnson Museum of Art.* Zarnowski (1938) attributes it to Girolamo di Tiziano, as the version in the New York Metropolitan Museum (cf. note to the preceding picture); Wehle (1940) considers it an authentic Titian, as Pallucchini does rather doubtfully, dating the portrait probably after 1559. Reproduced in *Johnson Collection, Two Hundred and Eighty-eight Paintings*, Philadelphia, 1953, p. 74.

Plate 175

VENUS. *Canvas, 115 × 67. Venice, Galleria Franchetti at Ca' d'Oro.* Signed: TITIANVS. Mutilated on the right side: about 20 cm. missing. Poglayen Neuwall (1934 and 1947) considers it to be by Titian's workshop; Berenson and Tietze both omit it from their catalogs. After its 1958 restoration, this picture appears to be of a sufficiently high quality to partly justify the Titian attribution proposed by A. Venturi, Suida, Fogolari (1935) and Wulff (1941).

It may therefore be a partly original version of the type of "*Venus pudica sola,*" according to Poglayen Neuwall's classification (1934)—and, in fact, the curtain (to the left instead of the right of the female figure) suggests the possibility that in the portion of the painting now missing one or two cherubs were depicted (cf. also note to plate 62).

Plate 176

VENUS BLINDFOLDING CUPID. *Canvas, 121.8 × 96.6. Washington, D.C., National Gallery of Art, Kress Collection, 1950.* Formerly in the Kenloss Collection in Scotland and the M.G. Close Smith Collection, Baycott Manor, Buckingham. Suida (1952) considers it to be the first original version, dating from about 1555, of the group on the left of the Borghese painting in Rome (plate 114). Pallucchini accepts it as an authentic Titian, advancing the date of its execution, however, to about 1560; while Della Pergola, doubting whether this painting really is by Titian himself, quite rightly considers it to be a replica of the Borghese picture. Berenson does not include it in his 1957 lists.

Plate 177

ST JEROME. *Canvas, 137.5 × 97. Lugano, Thyssen Collection.* From an English private collection. Suida was the first to publish this painting as an authentic Titian, and the attribution is accepted by O. Fischel, G. Gronau, L. von Hadeln, A. L. Mayer and A. Venturi, who date the canvas about twenty years after the Brera *St Jerome* reproduced in plate 65 (R. J. Heinemann, *Sammlung Schloss Rohoncz,* Lugano, 1958). Berenson includes it in his 1957 lists; Tietze does not mention it.

Plate 178

CHRIST GIVING HIS BLESSING. *Canvas, 96.5 × 80.5. Leningrad, Hermitage.* Purchased in 1850 from the Barbarigo Collection. Cavalcaselle places it among Titian's last works; Fischel dates it 1560–65; Suida also considers it a genuine Titian. The most recent criticism has tended to consider it as coming from Titian's workshop, although L. Venturi's harsh opinion (1912) of the work as very mediocre is not generally subscribed to. It does not appear in either Tietze's or Berenson's lists. Other variations, thought by some critics to be by Titian himself, of the same subject are to be found in the Vienna Kunsthistorisches Museum (83 × 61) and in the possession of the Earl of Darnley, shown at the 1960 Royal Academy Exhibition in London.

Plate 179

ST MARY MAGDALENE. *Canvas, 125 × 99. Naples, Capodimonte.* Bears an inscription written over the original one: "TITIANVS P.". Listed in the 1680 inventory of Palazzo del Giardino in Parma (Campori). Gronau believes this to be the canvas mentioned by Titian in one of his 1567 letters to Cardinal Farnese; it is certainly one of the many replicas painted by Titian's workshop of the lost original sent to Philip II. While Pallucchini sees the intervention of Titian in the landscape section, Tietze and Berenson both omit the picture from their lists. A recent restoration (1960) has confirmed the mediocre quality of this painting. (For the many replicas of this subject, see Lost Paintings, 1561, *St Mary Magdalene.*)

ST MARY MAGDALENE. *Canvas, 105 × 92. Busto Arsizio, Paolo Candiani Collection.* A good replica of the

Hermitage *Magdalene* (plate 112), it is considered by Arslan (1952) to be an authentic Titian, while Berenson (1957) omits it from his Titian catalogue. Reproduced in *The Burlington Magazine*, 1952, p. 306.

ST MARY MAGDALENE. *Canvas, 109 × 94. London, Colnaghi Collection.* Formerly in the collection of Lord Yarborough; listed as No. 102 in Christie's July 12, 1929 sale in London; then in the Gutekunst Collection. Mayer (1930) thinks it is an authentic Titian; Pallucchini judges it a good quality painting and considers it to be another version, with differences in the face and landscape, of the Leningrad canvas (plate 112). Neither Tietze nor Berenson mentions it. Reproduced in *Pantheon*, 1930, p. 145.

ST MARY MAGDALENE. *Canvas, 105.5 × 93. Malibu, California, J. Paul Getty Museum.* Not inferior in quality to the replicas painted by Titian's workshop of the Leningrad picture which are in the Candiani Collection in Busto Arsizio and in the Colnaghi Collection in London (see notes to the preceding paintings), it is included in Berenson's catalogue of Titian's paintings (1957).

ST MARY MAGDALENE. *Canvas, 114 × 99. Stuttgart, Staatsgalerie.* Signed: TITIANVS P. Formerly in the possession of Antonio Canova, then in the Barbini-Breganze Collection. Acquired for the Staatsgalerie in 1852. According to Gombosi (1937), this is a seventeenth-century copy from the time of Padovanino; Suida (1957 *Catalogue of the Gallery*) believes it to be an authentic Titian; however, most critics quite rightly take it to be a replica painted by Titian's workshop of the Leningrad picture (see above).

Plate 180

ST CATHERINE OF ALEXANDRIA. *Canvas, 119 × 99.5. Boston, Museum of Fine Arts.* Formerly in the Koppel Collection in Berlin. Fischel, Suida and Berenson all consider this an authentic Titian; Gronau (1936–37) thinks it is the canvas Titian sent to Cardinal Michele di Bonelli (1541–98) in 1567, and which the artist mentioned in his December 10 letter of that year to Cardinal Farnese (cf. Lost Paintings, 1567, *Mary Magdalene*; *St Peter the Martyr*; *St Catherine*). Tietze-Conrat (1954) identifies this canvas with that of 1567, listed as a work by Titian in the 1598 inventory of Cardinal Bonelli, and supposes it to be a *St Catherine of Siena* from 1520 transformed into a *St Catherine of Alexandria* about 1560. Tietze does not include it in his Titian catalog.

ST MARGARET. *Canvas, 116.5 × 98. Florence, Uffizi.* Longhi (1925), followed by Suida, considers this to be a late work by Titian; Tietze-Conrat (1946) believes it was painted by his workshop; while Tietze thinks the traditional attribution to Palma Giovane is more appropriate. Another version, mediocre in quality, of this painting is to be found in the Prado in Madrid. Reproduced in *L'Arte*, 1925, p. 46.

Plate 181

CHRIST AND SIMON OF CYRENE. *Canvas, 89.5 × 77. Leningrad, Hermitage.* Came in 1850 by purchase from the Barbarigo Collection. L. Venturi (1912) considers it to be a replica painted by Titian's school of the Prado painting (plate 127). It has been more or less ignored by art critics, and since its recent restoration (P. J. Kostrov, in *Ermitage, Restauration*, 1955) appears to be only slightly inferior in quality to the Madrid version.

ECCE HOMO. *Canvas, 95 × 89. Leningrad, Hermitage.* Came by purchase from the Barbarigo Collection. Cavalcaselle—followed by Fischel, among others—believes it to be an authentic late Titian; but most critics recently have considered it painted by Titian's workshop, and it does not appear in either Tietze's or Berenson's lists. Reproduced in *Klassiker der Kunst, Titian,* 1906, p. 168.

Plate 182

CHRIST ON THE CROSS AND THE GOOD THIEF. *Canvas, 137 × 149. Bologna, Pinacoteca.* Came in 1882 with the Zambeccari bequest. Fragment of a larger painting (E. Mauceri, 1931). Thode (1901), E. Van der Bercken and A. L. Mayer (*Jacopo Tintoretto,* Munich, 1923) attribute it to Tintoretto; according to Suida (1930–31) it is probably the remaining fragment of the Crucifixion for Giovanni d'Anna which Vasari saw in Titian's studio while it was being painted (cf. Lost Paintings, 1566). It was exhibited as an authentic Titian at the 1935 Venice Exhibition, the Amsterdam and Brussels Exhibitions in 1953–54, and the Paris Exhibition in 1954, and Berenson still lists it as such in his 1957 catalogs. Tietze has deleted it from his Titian lists. It is very close to Palma Giovane's style.

SUPPOSED PORTRAIT OF CATERINA CORNARO. *Canvas, 124 × 79. Vienna, Kunsthistorisches Museum.* Long ago attributed to Veronese and to Tintoretto; Engerth (1882) suggested it was close to the style of Titian; Longhi (1927) attributed it to Titian's last period, after which Wickhoff and Berenson have suggested the name of A. Badile. This painting does not appear in the Titian catalogs of either Tietze or Berenson. Reproduced in *Vita Artistica,* 1927, p. 225.

PORTRAIT OF A GENTLEMAN. *Canvas, 58.4 × 43.3. London, private collection.* The attribution of this painting (Borenius, 1942) to Titian's very last period has not been accepted by art critics. Reproduced in *The Burlington Magazine,* 1942, p. 132.

PORTRAIT OF GIOVANNI ANDREA DORIA. *Canvas, 200 × 104. Florence, Contini Bonacossi Collection.* Dated 1571, it is identifiable for Suida on the basis of a small portrait in the collection of the Archduke Ferdinand of the Tyrol. The painting, which has been hardly taken into consideration at all by art critics, is believed by Suida (1952) to be contemporary with the supposed portrait of Selim II in the Brass Collection in Venice (cf. note to plate 106). Suida also advances the hypothesis that the two portraits were commissioned by the same person, and believes that they formed part of a whole group of paintings—among them the big canvas in the Prado (plate 131) which was executed as a record of the victory of Lepanto. Reproduced in Suida, Plate CCLXXIV.

Plate 183

ECCE HOMO. *Canvas, 100 × 100. Madrid, Prado.* Listed in the Escorial in 1574 as a painting by Titian, to whom Cavalcaselle attributes it. Berenson considers it a youthful imitation of Titian by Jacopo Bassano; however, most contemporary critics believe it was painted by Titian's workshop (Pallucchini) or by one of his imitators, in connection with the painting in the St. Louis Museum (plate 135)—from which the late copies in the Dresden Gallery, in Burgos Cathedral, and at Hampton Court also derive (Tietze).

Plate 184

THE MADONNA OF PITY. *Canvas, 154 × 144. Florence, Pitti Palace.* Came to Florence in 1631 with the Della Rovere bequest. Commissioned in 1573 by the Duke of Urbino, whom Titian promised that he would paint the picture himself (Gronau, 1936). Gronau and Tietze-Conrat (1946)—who believes the picture to be an authentic Titian—have shown that the family gathered together under the Virgin's cloak is Titian's, not the Duke of Urbino's—as Dewnistoun (1909) had already suggested. In spite of the documentation of this painting, it is by Titian's workshop, Marco Vecellio certainly having had a hand in it—while Titian himself may have done some of the details.

Plate 185

SPAIN COMES TO THE AID OF RELIGION. *Canvas, 168 × 172.* *Rome, Doria Gallery.* Generally considered to be an old copy of the Prado painting in Madrid reproduced here as plate 130 (Suida; R. Wittkower, 1930–40); Tietze-Conrat (1951), however, believes she can identify it as the model for the picture begun for Alfonso I d'Este (see note to plate 130), from which Titian painted a first version—*Virtue and Peace Coming to the Aid of Religion*—for the Emperor Maximilian II, which was engraved by Giulio Fontana and mentioned in the correspondence between the Emperor himself and Veit von Dornberg, his representative in Venice, and which has now disappeared (cf. Lost Paintings, before 1568, *Allegory of Religion*, and Biographical Notes, 1568)—and a second version for Philip II. This painting in the Doria Gallery, which Pallucchini considers to be a replica painted by Titian's workshop, is not mentioned in Berenson's 1957 lists.

LOCATION OF PAINTINGS

ANCONA

CHURCH OF SAN DOMENICO
*The Crucifixion, with the Virgin,
SS Dominic and John* (plate 74).

ASCOLI PICENO

PINACOTECA
Stigmatization of St Francis (plates
100 and 101).

BALTIMORE

MUSEUM OF ART
Portrait of a Man (plate 95).

BERLIN

STAATLICHE MUSEEN
*Venus, Cupid, an Organist and a
Little Dog* (plate 34).
Girl with Dish of Fruit (plate 63).
Self-Portrait (plate 98).

BESANÇON

MUSÉE DES BEAUX-ARTS
*Portrait of Nicolas Perrenot Gran-
vella* (plate 26).

BOSTON

ISABELLA STEWART GARDNER
MUSEUM
The Rape of Europa (plate 88).

CAMBRIDGE, ENGLAND

FITZWILLIAM MUSEUM
Venus and a Lute Player (plate 73).
Tarquin and Lucretia (plate 136).

CINCINNATI

MUSEUM OF ART
Portrait of Philip II (plate 42).

DETROIT

INSTITUTE OF ARTS
Portrait of a Man with Flute (plate
94).
Judith (plate 117).

DRESDEN

GEMÄLDEGALERIE
Portrait of a Girl (plate 61).
Portrait of a Man with Palm
(plate 96).
Portrait of Lavinia (plate 97).

EDINBURGH

NATIONAL GALLERY OF SCOT-
LAND
Diana and Actaeon (plate 84).
Diana and Callisto (plate 85).

ESCORIAL

MONASTERY OF ST LAWRENCE
St Margaret and the Dragon (plate
52).
St Jerome (plate 75).
The Adoration of the Magi (plate 76).
Christ in the Garden of Gethsemane
(plate 104a).
The Last Supper (plate 105).
The Crucifixion (plates 110 and
111).
The Martyrdom of St Lawrence
(plate 121).

FLORENCE

UFFIZI
Venus, Cupid and a Little Dog
(plate 35).
Portrait of Ludovico Beccadelli (plate
47a).

GENEVA

IN A PRIVATE COLLECTION
Portrait of Giovanni da Castaldo (plate 28).

KANSAS CITY

GALLERY OF ART
Portrait of Antonio Perrenot Granvella (plate 27).

KASSEL

GEMÄLDEGALERIE
Portrait of a Gentleman (plates 40 and 41).

KROMIERIZ

NATIONAL GALLERY
The Punishment of Marsyas (plate 143).

LENINGRAD

HERMITAGE
Danaë (plate 59).
St Mary Magdalene (plate 112).
St Sebastian (plates 132 and 133).

LENTIAI (BELLUNO)

PARISH CHURCH
St Titian (plate 36).

LILLE

MUSÉE DES BEAUX-ARTS
The Stoning of St Stephen (plate 83).

LONDON

WALLACE COLLECTION
Perseus and Andromeda (plate 89).

NATIONAL GALLERY
Votive Portrait of the Vendramin Family (plates 14–19).
Venus and Adonis (plate 56).
Diana and Actaeon (plate 87) on loan from the Earl of Harewood.
The Tribute Money (plate 126)
Madonna and Child (plate 139).

PRIVATE COLLECTION
Allegory of Prudence (plate 120).

LUGANO

THYSSEN COLLECTION
Portrait of Antonio Anselmi (plate 39).
Portrait of the Doge Francesco Venier (plates 50 and 51).

MADRID

PRADO
Ecce Homo (plate 20).
Portrait of Charles V at the Battle of Mühlberg (plates 22–24).
Portrait of Isabella of Portugal (plate 25).
Prometheus (plate 30).
Sisyphus (plate 31).
Venus, Cupid and an Organist (plate 32).
Venus and an Organist (plate 33).
Mater Dolorosa (plate 37).
Portrait of Philip II (plates 43, 44.)
Supposed Portrait of a Knight of Malta (plate 45).
The Adoration of the Holy Trinity (plate 53).
Bust of Christ (plate 54).
Mater Dolorosa (plate 55).
Venus and Adonis (plate 57).
Danaë (plate 58).
The Entombment (plate 79).
Salome (plate 82).
Christ in the Garden of Gethsemane (plate 104b).
St Margaret and the Dragon (plate 113).
The Entombment (plate 124).
Christ Carrying the Cross (plate 127).
Self-Portrait (plate 128).
The Fall of Man (plate 129).
Spain Coming to the Aid of Religion (plate 130).
Philip II Offering the Infante Don Fernando to Victory (plate 131).

MEDOLE (MANTUA)

CHURCH OF SANTA MARIA
The Risen Christ Appearing to His Mother (plate 64).

MELBOURNE

NATIONAL GALLERY OF VICTORIA
Portrait of a Franciscan Monk (plate 47b).

MILAN

AMBROSIANA
The Adoration of the Magi (plates 77 and 78).
BRERA
St Jerome in the Wilderness (plate 65).

MUNICH

BAYERISCHE STAATSGEMÄLDESAMMLUNGEN
Portrait of Charles V (plate 21).
Madonna and Child (plate 99).
The Crown of Thorns (plate 134).

NAPLES

CAPODIMONTE (NATIONAL GALLERY)
Pope Paul III and His Grandsons Alessandro and Ottavio Farnese (plate 1 and color plate I).
Pope Paul III Wearing the Papal Cap (plate 2).
Portrait of Cardinal Alessandro Farnese (plate 3).
Danaë (plates 4–5).
Portrait of a Girl (plate 6).
Portrait of Pier Luigi Farnese (plate 7).
Portrait of Cardinal Pietro Bembo (plate 10).
Portrait of Philip II (plate 48).

CHURCH OF SAN DOMENICO MAGGIORE
The Annunciation (plate 71).

NEW YORK

FRICK COLLECTION
Portrait of Pietro Aretino (plate 11).

METROPOLITAN MUSEUM
Venus and Adonis (plate 91).
Venus with the Lute Player (plate 72).

PIEVE DI CADORE

ARCHDIACONATE
Madonna and Child between SS Titian and Andrew (plate 125).

ROME

BORGHESE GALLERY
Venus Blindfolding Cupid (or *The Education of Cupid*) (plates 114–116).
St Dominic (plate 118).
Christ at the Column (plate 119).

ROTTERDAM

BOYMANS MUSEUM
Child with Dogs (plate 140).

ST LOUIS

ART MUSEUM
Ecce Homo (plate 135).

SAN FRANCISCO

DE YOUNG MEMORIAL MUSEUM
Portrait of a Friend of Titian (plate 46b).

SERRAVALLE (VENETO)

DUOMO
Madonna and Child in Glory, and SS Peter and Paul (plate 12).

STOCKHOLM

RASCH COLLECTION
Portrait of Philip II (plate 49).

VENICE

ACCADEMIA
The Deposition (plates 144–146).

BRASS COLLECTION
Portrait of an Oriental Potentate
(plate 106).

CHURCH OF THE JESUITS
The Martyrdom of St Lawrence
(plates 66–69).

CHURCH OF SAN LIO
St James of Compostella (plate 13).

CHURCH OF SAN SALVATORE
The Transfiguration (plate 103).
The Annunciation (plates 108 and
109).

CHURCH OF SAN SEBASTIANO
St Nicholas of Bari (plate 107).

CHURCH OF SANTA MARIA
DELLA SALUTE
Pentecost (plate 70).

DUCAL PALACE
*The Doge Antonio Grimani Before
Faith* (plate 102).

SANSOVINIANA LIBRARY
Wisdom (plates 80 and 81).

VIENNA

AKADEMIE DER BILDENDEN
KUNST
Tarquin and Lucretia (plates 137 and
138).

KUNSTHISTORISCHES MUSEUM
*Portrait of a Man with Book and
Staff* (plate 8).
Portrait of a Boy (plate 9).
Portrait of John Frederick of Saxony
(plate 29).
Supposed Portrait of Benedetto Varchi
(plate 38).
Danaë (plate 60).
Diana and Callisto (plate 86).
Portrait of Fabrizio Salvaresio
(plates 92 and 93).
Portrait of Jacopo Strada (plates
122 and 123).
Nymph and Shepherd (plates 141 and
142).

WASHINGTON, D.C.

CORCORAN GALLERY OF ART
Portrait of Martino Pasqualigo
(plate 46a).

NATIONAL GALLERY OF ART
Venus with a Mirror (plate 62).
Venus and Adonis (plate 90).

SELECTED CRITICISM

To Titian alone belongs the glory of perfect coloring. Either none of the old painters possessed this art—or, if they did, modern painters, in greater or lesser degree, lack it. Therefore, as I have already said, he (Titian) progresses on a par with Nature: every figure he paints lives, and moves, and pulses as in the flesh. This artist has not shown superficial charm in his works, but instead a rightness of colors; not affected ornamentation, but a masterly firmness; not crudeness, but the softness and gentleness of Nature. In his paintings the play of light and shade is such as Nature herself reveals, hiding and diminishing objects. . . .

L. DOLCE,
Dialogo della Pittura, 1557.

He (Titian) painted the panel on the altar of St Peter the Martyr in the Church of SS Giovanni and Paolo, depicting the martyred saint more than life-size, in a grove of huge trees. He has fallen to the ground and is being attacked with great ferocity by a soldier who has wounded him in the head; he is half-dead, so that in his face can be seen the horror of death—while the face of another monk who is fleeing expresses the fear and terror of death. In the air there are two nude angels coming from a streak of lightning which illuminates the landscape. This landscape is very beautiful, as is the entire picture, being the most successful, the most well-known, and the greatest work—as well as being the best understood and carried out—that Titian has painted up to this time . . . .

However, it is true that the way of painting which Titian has used in these last-mentioned pictures ("poesies" for Philip II) is very different from his youthful way of painting. His early paintings were carried out with a certain fineness and incredible diligence, to be viewed from either near to, or from a distance; these later ones are carried out with brushstrokes which are coarsely applied, and with blobs of color, in such a way that while from near to the pictures are impossible to look at, from a distance they seem perfect. . . . This way of painting is judicious, beautiful, and truly marvelous in that it makes the paintings live, and look as though they are executed with great art, hiding the hard work that went into them.

G. VASARI,
The Lives. . ., 1568.

But among them all—not only Italian painters but painters all over the world—Titian shines like a sun among little stars, as much on account of his human figures as of his landscapes, making himself the equal of Apelles who was the first inventor of thunder-claps, rains, winds, the sun, lightning and storms. And, particularly, this Titian has colored in the most delightful way mountains, plains, trees, woods, shadows, light, inundations of the sea and rivers, earthquakes, stones, animals, and everything else which pertains to landscape painting.

And his representations of flesh have so much beauty and grace by means of his color mixture and tints that the flesh seems real and alive, especially the plumpness and tenderness which one naturally sees in his paintings. He has shown this same felicity in giving color to silk, velvet and brocade cloths, to various breast-plates and shields, to coats-of-armor, and other similar objects. . . .

G. P. LOMAZZO,
Idea del Tempio della pittura, 1590.

Titian was truly the most excellent of all painters, because his brushes always gave birth to expressions of life. Giacomo Palma Giovane said to me . . . that Titian based his pictures on a great mass of colors, which served (one might say) as a base for whatever he was going to paint over it; and I myself have seen his determined brushstrokes laden with color, sometimes of a streak of pure earth red which served him (one might say) as a half-tone; other times with a brushstroke of white lead; and with the same brush colored with red, black and yellow, he formed a highlight; and with these rules of technique made the promise of an excellent figure appear in four brushstrokes.

After having laid these important foundations, he then used to turn the pictures to the wall, and leave them—sometimes for as long as several months—without looking at them; and when he wanted to apply his brush to them again, he would examine them most rigorously, as though they had been his greatest enemies, in order to see whether he could find any defects in them, or discover anything which would not be in harmony with the delicacy of his intentions—just as a good surgeon cares for his patient, seeing whether it is necessary to narrow down a swelling, or an overabundance of flesh, straightening an arm here (if the bone structure was not just right), a foot there if it is at a wrong angle, lengthening it, without thought for the pain—and so on. Working thus, and redesigning his figures, Titian brought them into a perfect symmetry which could represent the beauty of Art as well as of Nature. After this was done, he put his hand to some other picture until the first was dry, working in the same way with this other; thus gradually he covered those quintessential outlines of figures with living flesh, making many replicas of them which only lacked breath to be truly alive. He never painted a figure all at once, and used to say that he who improvises his song can form neither learned nor well-turned verses. But the final polish of the last finishing touches was to unite now and then by a touch of his fingers the extremes of the light areas, so that they became almost half-tints, and uniting one tint to another; at other times, with a stroke he would place a dark streak in a corner, to reinforce it he would also put a streak of red, like a drop of blood, which invigorated any superficial feeling there might be. Thus continuing, he made perfect his animated figures. Palma told me that it was quite true that Titian, in the final phase of his paintings, painted more with his fingers than with his brushes.

M. BOSCHINI,
Le Ricche Miniere della pittura veneziana, 1674.

The colors on Titian's palette were few, and were ordinary ones; therefore, the great beauty of his paintings was born of contrasts. . . . A pure white cloth next to a nude figure shows up the flesh tints to such an extent that they seem to be modelled with the most vivid vermilions—whereas in actual fact Titian has used nothing but the most ordinary earth red with a little varnish towards the contours and the edges. Other very dark objects, of intense colors—and sometimes even of black—give the same effect: and as well as beautifying the colors near them, each sphere of color gives great force to his figures which, as we have said already, were painted only with merging half-tints, without deep shadows. Thus it was that the beauty of Titian's paintings never surpassed the truth, and they both were and still are universally admired especially since they are at one with the great principle of Nature.

A. M. ZANETTI,
Della pittura veneziana e delle opere pubbliche de' Veneziani maestri, 1771.

Titian is one of those men who most draw near to the spirit of the ancients . . . in all the others one would say there is a grain of madness: only he is balanced and master of himself, of his accomplishments, and of his dexterity which never dominates him and of which he does not make a show.

He moves one, I believe, not by the depth of his expression nor by his grasp of his subject, but by his simplicity and lack of affectation. In his work, pictorial qualities are brought to their highest point; what he paints, is painted; eyes look and are animated by the fire of life. Life and reason are apparent everywhere.

E. DELACROIX,
Journal, 1834 and 1857.

At the center of the Venetian school stands the powerful figure of Titian . . . Titian, who in the almost one hundred years of his life represented or created or revealed in exemplary fashion to the younger generations everything that Venice was capable of inventing in the world of painting. . . .

The divine spark in Titian is such that he attributes to Man and to objects that harmony of existence which, according to their nature, should be contained within them and which already lives within them, even though obscurely and without really being apparent. Everything which in reality is disunited, dispersed, accidental, he represents as complete, free, happy. . . .

This is abundantly clear in his portraits . . . before which one almost always forgets to ask oneself how, with only a basis of fleeting, hidden traits to work on, the master has managed to give life to such imposing beings.

J. BURCKHARDT,
Der Cicerone, 1855.

Titian, in spite of a sturdier, less refined nature, did nothing for a generation after Giorgione's death but work on his lines. A difference in quality between the two masters shows itself from the first, but the spirit that animated each is identical. The pictures Titian was painting ten years after his companion's death have not only many of the qualities of Giorgione's, but something more, as if done by an older Giorgione, with better possession of himself and with a larger and firmer hold on the world. At the same time, they show no diminution of spontaneous joy of life, and even an increased sense of its value and dignity. . . . In fact, the old Titian was, in his way of painting, remarkably like some of the best French masters of the end of the nineteenth century. This makes him only the more attractive, particularly when with handling of this kind he combined the power of creating forms of beauty such as he has given us in the *Wisdom* of the Venetian Library of San Marco or in the *Shepherd and Nymph* of Vienna. The difference between the old Titian, author of these works, and the young Titian, painter of the *Assumption* and of the *Bacchus and Ariadne*, is the difference between the Shakespeare of the *Midsummer Night's Dream* and the Shakespeare of the *Tempest*. Titian and Shakespeare begin and end so much in the same way by no mere accident. They were both products of the Renaissance, they underwent similar changes, and each was the highest and completest expression of his own age.

B. BERENSON,
Italian Painters of the Renaissance, 1897.

In Titian's paintings, his landscapes reveal a force of expression which art had not previously known. This was, no doubt, an innovation of Giorgione's, but—except in the *Tempest*—it is Titian who should be recognized mainly as the innovator in those pictures where, as in the Dresden *Venus*, for example, Nature with all her penetrating poetry amplifies the nude splendor of the Venuses: Nature, for Titian was always more than just a simple visual ornamentation. The more sensitive landscape artists—such as Gentile Bellini, or Carpaccio—took pleasure in noting in minute detail the picturesque fantasies light plays on buildings and on water, but then they proceeded to put in their foregrounds little figures which appear indifferent to the seductions of such sights. How different is the role of Nature in Titian's pictures! It is true that, in the Padua frescoes, the landscape is still merely episodic with the aim of being pleasing to the eye; but even so, in *The Jealous Husband*, it adds a note of terror that serves the drama, which needs just such a landscape for ambush, for dagger thrusts: the savage rock-faces throw a tragic shadow on the crime being enacted beneath them.

From then onwards, Titian evoked with extraordinary ability, through his choice of place and lighting, the exact impression that the scenes he described wanted to produce. His landscapes have a soul.

L. HOURTICQ,
La Jeunesse de Titien, 1919.

The motive force, the special energy of color, which has become more than a mere coloring ingredient or a means of registering sensitive perception, he (Titian) transforms, one might say, into an intangible fluid, into an autonomous factor capable of arousing, even by itself and independently of the linear-plastic composition of the picture, that spiritual participation which represents for us the most important characteristic of the new art. In this way, among Titian's last works we find pictures which do not try to be anything other than chromatic symphonies, and it would be childish to want to measure them by the yardstick of naturalistic or academic drawing. The color, in which the richnesses of an inexhaustible palette are put together in an effect which is almost monochrome, vibrates like a living creature in unison with the spectator's sensitivity. This emancipation of the expressive value of color has opened up a number of new possibilities to painting: to it we owe a large part of the effects made by the art of Baroque composition, effects stretched to the furthest limits of the imagination. The experience thus obtained determined the path of that exaggerated painting which sees its own main aim in the representation of naturalistic color processes. In this way, too, the new idealism has opened up new possibilities to a subsequent naturalism.

M. DVORAK,
Storia dell'Arte Italiana, 1929

Together with the other great masters of the High Renaissance, Titian founded the era of "Belle Arti," and with it inaugurated a reign of art, independent of and superior to reality because of its power. But since his personal role in this raising of art to a higher, more noble plane is to be found in the vigor of his perception and in the naturalness of his vision, he more than any other artist has contributed to making artistic beauty a general need of the intellect. It was not by chance that he was the favorite painter of the princely courts, and given the title of painter to an emperor: thanks to Titian, art became a sign of social distinction, an essential part of a common culture, and the successor to other spiritual forces about to disappear. This conception of art prevailed until the middle of the nineteenth century, and its last corollaries have made themselves felt up to the threshold of our own time; he whose work made concrete this ideal merits the highest of places in the history of the development of the human spirit. Titian is not only a great painter: he is equally—just because he did not intend to be other than a great painter—a historical phenomenon of very marked significance.

H. TIETZE,
Tizian, 1936.

Titian's entire activity is marked by a continual growing in depth of expressive values, functioning in a freshness which is continually renewed by inspiration. Delacroix's comment that "Il obéit à chaque instant à une émotion vraie, il faut qu'il rend cette émotion" sums up neatly the miracle by which each of his works is a new cosmos; one does not find him taking pleasure in a device, or a formula, or an attitude already arrived at. Each genuinely authentic work (and in this field philological criticism still has a good deal of work to do) is necessary to Titian's story: in each one of them his feeling takes shape with a certain newness, with a different and always renewed aim. In the portraits, which would seem more bound to an external reality or to a label, his inspiration shows his continual impatience with clichés and with any thematic or formal situation which has already been dealt with. Only an intense feeling for humanity could provide Titian the tremendous vitality of his taste and could make itself felt in the multiple facets of his art.

R. PALLUCCHINI,
La Pittura Veneziana del Cinquecento, 1944.

The young Titian does away completely with the timidity of Giorgione. To this end he suppresses the *stumatura* inherited from artists before Raphael, and goes back to study the local fifteenth-century painters, on Bellini and Carpaccio. This is clearly shown in the Antwerp picture which seems so archaic. For the same reason the sublime Padua frescoes of 1511 seem as though they were painted by a modern Piero. In their contrasts between masses of light and shadow, the shadow comes through as "tone" and is transposed to the ideal plane of color; it becomes part of the picture, that is to say, without a plastic leap, without the use of chiaroscuro, without the blending of color, in the satisfying harmony of "chromatic depth." Nevertheless, even the moving classicism of Giorgione serves an aim, now that the uniting of forms no longer comes about by means of volumes and almost crystalline planes as in Antonello, Bellini and Carpaccio— that is, only by placing, or juxtaposition—but by mature "composition" of free, significant gestures, in, I would say, almost a spatial curve. Bodies are delineated as in an imaginary ancient Greek picture which has suddenly acquired the power of moving into space three-dimensionally. I am thinking of the two Este pictures with the *Bacchanal* and the *Festival of the Cupids*, of Lord Ellesmere's *Three Ages*, and I become aware of the fact that Florence and Rome would never otherwise have known how to relive a long-dreamed classicism. All in all, the young Titian is truly somewhat Phidias-like: his color mixture itself has the living warmth of Greek marble, and the same sublimated, faultless sensuality in comparison with the too heavy, flagrant sensuality of the late Giorgione. I have said that the figures delineate themselves: the delineation is merely sketched and it is just at the limits of every chromatic zone that Titian leaves the breathing space of a changeable sketch, of an altering, growing, living thing. Delicate, fleeting wrinkles, burning patches, slight liquefyings, vivid touches which bring to mind the painful scars of Cézanne when he was trying to *réaliser*—Titian brings off all these without difficulty. This is taking place in Venice, while in Rome, Raphael is painting the *Stanze*, and Michelangelo, stiff-necked and cursing, is finishing the Sistine Chapel ceiling. . . . How Titian then, and for almost a quarter of a century up to about 1545, fought with varying outcome against the "Etruscan demons" who were converging on Venice from every side, is a story which . . . left its mark on almost every one of his paintings during those years: the *Bacchus and Ariadne*, a work to please Rubens rather than the Greek classicists; the *St Sebastian* of the Brescia triptych; parts of the Pesaro altarpiece which were models for Van Dyck; the famous lost *St Peter the Martyr* in San Zanipolo; the heavy *St John the Baptist* in the Accademia; the bombastic *Flagellation* in the Louvre—which was, together with the Vienna *Ecce Homo*, a model for Rubens; and, finally, that ceiling in Santo Spirito, now in the Louvre, which Boschini lauded (possibly because he saw in it a prelude to Tintoretto's inflated figures) in the following lines: "O what beautifully big shapes! O what great forms! What proud, vivacious movements in perspective!"—a cry which leaves us cold.

It is just this evidence which does not allow us to accept the date of 1537—that is to say in the midst of the crisis (even if this was interrupted for a moment by the archaic banality of the *Presentation at the Temple*)—for the execution of the *St John the Almsgiver*, which already contains the noble resolution of the long discord, around 1545.

In contrast to the innocent candor of St Mark which shines forth from the youthful altarpiece in the Salute, what moral haughtiness, what stubborn sovereignty! Florence and Rome have by now convinced Titian that humanity, even in the figure of a beggar, is unable to act except by being invested with dignity and power; but the more suppressedly violent are the gestures (here a deliberate contrast between reading and charity), the more Titian makes them seem contrived, attacking them from every side with his whiplashes of air and of dark and sliding light, in what I would call a sort of chromatic flagellation.

When one thinks of the easy compromise between formal elegance and color that Schiavone adopted during that same period, one can better realize the depths in which Titian—implicated in this drama which grew out of painting itself—was groping. Ancient form was an irrecuperable myth, the pregnant memory of lost power, long wrapped in cosmic veiling, chaotic as in the San Salvatore *Annunciation*, one of the most desperate in all art, where the room is filled as though with a half-spent apocalyptic fire which speckles and stains the figures, presenting them in a sort of "magic impressionism." And the apocalypse is followed up in the specters and hallucinations of El Greco.

R. LONGHI,
Viatico per Cinque Secoli di Pittura Veneziana, 1946.

Titian's Mannerist experiences, deepened and resolved before his stay in Rome, were to be concluded in a heroic exaltation of the individual, in so far as the individual is a knowing and active protagonist in history—even though he may be at the mercy of a destiny which may be adverse, and bound to his limited, arduous work. Far from denying the artist's previous activity, however, this attitude confirmed its essential reasons, since not even then was Man conceived according to an abstract anthropomorphic conception, isolated within himself and in opposition to Nature, but rather as the actual center of the cosmic life which flows in him. Here lay the possibility of bringing together in a personal vision the two greatest figurative traditions of the sixteenth century: the Venetian tradition, renewed by Giorgione, and the Florentine-Tuscan tradition; here also lay the possibility of re-establishing on a different, more mature, complex plane, that balance between feeling and humanistic rationalism, between civilization and Nature, which is the perennial basis of Titian's art.

G. A. DELL'ACQUA,
Tiziano, 1955.

BIBLIOGRAPHY

Titian's bibliography is very extensive, even taking into consideration the fact that a considerable part of it is comprised of articles dealing with paintings attributed to him. Aside from the best-known sources—Sanudo, Michiel, Aretino, Vasari, Ridolfi—the notes to each plate, when his is a major work, carry only the name of the author. These important works are: Cavalcaselle's wide-ranging monograph, still fundamental (C. B. Cavalcaselle and J. A. Crowe, *Tiziano, la sua vita e i suoi tempi*, Florence, 1877-78); the monographs of G. Gronau (*Tizian*, Berlin, 1900; London, 1904; Stuttgart, 1930) and C. Ricketts (*Titian*, London, 1910); D. von Hadeln's valuable comments in his edition of Ridolfi (Berlin, 1914); L. Hourticq's explanatory remarks on Titian's youthful activity (*La jeunesse de Titien*, Paris, 1919; *Le problème de Giorgione*, Paris, 1930); T. Hetzer's illuminating pages on Titian's color (*Tizian, Geschichte seiner Farbe*, Frankfurt, 1935; *Tizian,* Frankfurt, 1948); W. Suida's monograph, noteworthy for its collection of dates (*Tiziano*, Rome, 1933); H. Tietze's exemplary critical monograph (*Tizian, Leben und Werk*, Vienna, 1936, and the revised edition, 1950); R. Pallucchini's detailed profile (Bologna, 1953 and 1954); and G. A. Dell'Acqua's equally valuable profile which focuses in a highly sensitive synthesis the essence of Titian's art (*Tiziano*, Milan, 1955). D. Cecchi's book (*Tiziano*, Milan, 1955) should also be especially noted for its vivid evocations both of Titian himself and his historical background.

The other studies mentioned—among which those by the following authors are of particular importance either for their documented research, for new attributions of paintings to Titian, or for critical comments: Justi, Gronau, Von Hadeln, Borenius, Berenson, Longhi, Mayer, Suida, A. and L. Venturi, Fiocco, Tietze and Tietze-Conrat, and Morassi—are indicated in the text of both volumes with the author's name and publication date; in the bibliography which follows this note they are listed alphabetically according to author, and chronologically within the list of works of each author.

G. ADRIANI. *Anton van Dyck—Italienisches Skizzenbuch*, Vienna, 1941.

A. ALVAREZ CABANAS. *La Ultima Cena, cuadro de Tiziano existente en las capitulares de El Escorial*, Madrid, 1934.

ANONIMO DEL TIZIANELLO (G. M. VERDIZZOTTI?). *Breve Compendium della vita del famoso Titiano Vecelli di Cadore*, Venice, 1622.

ANONIMO MORELLIANO. See: Frizzoni, Michiel, I. Morelli.

F. ARCANGELI. "La 'Disputa' del Tintoretto a Milano," in *Paragone*, 1955.

P. ARETINO. *Lettere (1535-1537)*, Venice, 1551; Paris, 1609.

G. C. ARGAN. *L'amor sacro e l'amor profano*, Milan, 1954.

E. ARSLAN. "Un ritratto inedito di Tiziano," in *Dedalo*, 1931.

E. ARSLAN. *Il concetto di "luminismo" e la pittura veneta barocca*, Milan, 1946.

E. ARSLAN. "Titian's 'Magdalen'," in *The Burlington Magazine*, 1952.

J. BABELON. *Titien*, Paris, 1950.

L. BALDASS. "Ein unbekanntes Hauptwerk des Cariani," *in Oesterreichisches Jahrbuch*, N.F.3, 1929.

L. BALDASS. "Eine Porträtskizze vom jungen Tizian," in *Zeitschrift für Kunstwissenschaft*, 1955.

L. BALDASS. Zur Erforschung des "Giorgionismo" bei den Generationsgenossen Tizians," in *Jahrbuch der Kunsthistorischen Sammlungen in Wien*, 1961.

F. BALDINUCCI. *Notizie de' Professori del disegno*, Florence, 1681.

A. BANTI. *Lorenzo Lotto*, Florence, 1955.

C. BARFOED. *Tiziano Vecellio*, Copenhagen, 1889.

V. BASCH. *Titien*, Paris, 1918 (2nd ed., 1926).

W. BATHOE. *Catalogue of Charles I's collection*, London, 1757.

E. BATTISTI. "Disegni inediti di Tiziano e lo studio d'Alfonso d'Este," in *Commentari*, 1954.

R. BEER. "Akten, Register und Inventare aus dem 'Archivo General', zu Simancas," in *Jahrbuch der Sammlungen des a. h. Kaiserhauses*, XII, 2, 1891; XIV, 2, 1893; XIX, 2, 1899.

B. BEINERT. "Carlos Ven Mühlberg, de Tiziano" in *Archivo Español de Arte*, 1946.

M. BELL. *The Early Work of Titian*, London, 1905.

P. BEMBO. *Delle lettere di M.P. Bembo ai suoi conjunti ed amici*, Venice, 1564.

O. BENESCH. "Gemäldegalerie in Kremsier," in *Pantheon*, 1928.

O. BENESCH. "Titian and Tintoretto: Study in Comparative Criticism," in *Arte Veneta*, 1958.

E. VON DER BERCKEN. "Some Unpublished Works by Tintoretto and Titian," in *The Burlington Magazine*, 1924.

B. BERENSON. *The Venetian Painters of the Renaissance*, New York and London, 1894.

B. BERENSON. "Un portrait de Titien à Budapest," in *Gazette des Beaux-Arts*, 1926.

B. BERENSON. "While on Tintoretto," in *Festschrift für M. Friedländer*, Leipzig, 1927.

B. BERENSON. "The Missing Head of the Glasgow 'Christ and Adulteress'," in *Art in America*, 1928.

B. BERENSON. *Italian Pictures of the Renaissance*, Oxford, 1932.

B. BERENSON. "Notes on Giorgione," in *Arte Veneta*, 1954.

B. BERENSON. *Italian Pictures of the Renaissance—Venetian School*, London, 1957.

W. BERGMANN. *Tizian*, Hannover, 1865.

G. BERNARDINI. *Sebastiano del Piombo*, Bergamo, 1908.

P. BEROQUI. *Tizian en el Museo del Prado*, Madrid, 1927 (2nd ed., 1946).

E. BERTI TOESCA. "Per la Mostra di Tiziano a Venezia: quadri di Tiziano nell'Accademia di San Luca," in *Bollettino d'Arte*, 1934-35.

A. BERTOLOTTI. *Artisti veneti in Roma*, Venice, 1885.

J. BIALOSTOCKI. "The Empress Isabella, Titian and Guillim Scrots," in *Oud Holland*, II (1954).

Z. BICCHIERAI. *Lettere d'illustri Italiani non mai stampate...*, Florence, 1854.

G. BIERMANN. "Tizians 'Judith mit dem Haupt des Holofernes'," in *Der Cicerone*, 1929.

M. BIONDO. *Della nobilissima Pittura*, Venice, 1549.

G. BISCARO. "Di un affresco di Tiziano a Treviso," in *Gazzetta di Treviso,* January 1–2, 1898.

W. VON BODE. "Die 'Venus mit dem Orgelspieler' von Tiziano im Kaiser-Friedrich-Museum," in *Amtliche Berichte Berliner Museen,* 1917–18.

F. BOLOGNA. "La 'Sacra Conversazione' di Monaco. Argomenti per la restituzione d'un Tiziano," in *Paragone,* 1951.

F. BOLOGNA. "Un doppio ritratto di Tiziano, inedito," in *Arte Veneta,* 1957.

F. BOLOGNA and G. DORIA. *Mostra del Ritratto Storico Napoletano,* catalog, Naples, 1954.

G. M. BONOMI. *Il quadro di Tiziano della famiglia Martinengo Colleoni,* Bergamo, 1886.

T. BORENIUS. "The Venetian School . . .," in *The Burlington Magazine,* 1913.

T. BORENIUS. "Some Reflections on the Last Phase of Titian," in *The Burlington Magazine,* 1922.

T. BORENIUS. "A Masterpiece by Titian," in *Apollo,* 1928.

T. BORENIUS. "Two Pictures by Titian in the Escorial," in *The Burlington Magazine,* 1937.

T. BORENIUS. "A landscape by Titian," in *The Burlington Magazine,* 1938.

T. BORENIUS. "An Unknown Work of Titian's Last Phase," in *The Burlington Magazine,* 1942.

R. BORGHINI. *Il Riposo,* Florence, 1584.

A. BORROUGHS. *Art criticism from a Laboratory,* Boston, 1938.

D. BORTOLAN. *L'antica loggia del Palazzo del Capitanio in Vicenza,* Vicenza, 1892.

M. BOSCHINI. *La Carta del navegar pitoresco,* Venice, 1660.

M. BOSCHINI. *Le Ricche Minere della Pittura,* Venice, 1664 (2nd ed., 1674).

G. G. BOTTARI and S. TICOZZI. *Raccolta di lettere . . .,* Milan, 1822–25.

W. BRAGHIROLLI. "Tiziano alla Corte dei Gonzaga a Mantova," in *Atti e Memorie della R. Accademia Virgiliana di Mantova,* 1881.

P. BRANDOLESE. *Pitture ecc. di Padova nuovamente descritte . . .,* Padua, 1795.

W. BRAUNFELS. "Titian or Orazio Vecellio?", in *The Burlington Magazine,* 1957.

A. BRENDEL. "Interpretation of the 'Olkham Venus'," in *The Art Bulletin,* 1946.

C. BRIERE MISME. "La 'Danaë' de Rembrandt et son véritable sujet," in *Gazette des Beaux-Arts,* 1952.

A. M. BRIZIO. "Il Greco a Venezia," in *L'Arte,* 1932.

A. M. BRIZIO. "Tiziano" in *Grande Dizionario Enciclopedico,* ed. P. Fedele, Vol. X, Turin, 1939.

M. BRUNETTI. "Una figlia sconosciuta di Tiziano," in *Rivista di Venezia,* 1935.

M. BRUNETTI. "Una strana interpretazione del 'Concerto' della Galleria Pitti," in *Rivista di Venezia,* 1935.

M. BRUNETTI. *Il Fondaco nostro dei Tedeschi,* Venice, 1941.

F. BRUSTOLINI. "Tiziano Vecellio e la pala di Jacopo de' Pesaro ai Frari," in *Cronache d'Arte,* 1925.

L. BURCHARD. "Zwei Papstbildnisse Tizians," in *Jahrbuch der preuss. Kunstsammlungen,* 1925.

J. BURCKHARDT. *Der Cicerone,* Basel, 1855.

J. BURCKHARDT. *Beiträge zur Kunstgeschichte in Italien,* Basel, 1898, passim.

G. CADORIN. *Dello amore di Veneziani di Tiziano,* Venice, 1833.

G. CADORIN. *Dei tre quadroni dipinti da Tiziano per la sala del Palazzo pubblico di Brescia,* Venice, 1879.

M. CALVESI. "Il 'San Giorgio Cini' e Paolo Pino," in *Venezia e l'Europa,* Venice, 1956.

E. CALZINI. "Tiziano e i duchi d'Urbino," in *Rassegna bibliografica dell'arte italiana,* 1905.

G. CAMPORI. *Gli artisti italiani e stranieri negli stati estensi,* Modena, 1855 and 1863.

G. CAMPORI. *Lettere artistiche inedite,* Modena, 1866.

G. CAMPORI. *Raccolta di cataloghi ed inventari inediti . . .,* Modena, 1870.

G. CAMPORI. "Tiziano e gli Estensi," in *Nuova Antologia,* 1874.

E. CARLI. "Impressioni tizianesche alla mostra veneziana di Palazzo Pesaro," in *Vie dell'Impero,* 1935.

H. CARO-DELVAILLE. *Titien,* Paris, 1913.

G. CASTELFRANCO. "Tiziano," in *La riforma letteraria,* 1936–37.

G. B. CAVALCASELLE. "Spigolature tizianesche," in *Archivio Storico d'Arte,* 1891.

G. B. CAVALCASELLE and J. A. CROWE. *A History of Painting in North Italy,* London, 1871 and 1912.

G. B. CAVALCASELLE and J. A. CROWE. *Tiziano, la sua vita e i suoi tempi,* 2 vols., Florence, 1877–78. London, 1881.

E. CECCHI. *Tiziano,* Milan, 1955.

U. CHRISTOFFEL. *Tizian,* Stuttgart, 1957.

E. CICOGNA. *Iscrizione veneziana,* Venice, 1853, passim.

L. CICOGNARA. "Elogio di Tiziano Vecellio," in *Reggia Veneta Accademia di Belle Arti,* Venice, 1809.

G. CLAUSSE. *Les Farnèse,* Paris, 1905.

G. P. CLERICI. "Tiziano e la 'Hypnerotomachia Poliphili'," in *Bibliofilia,* 1918–19.

L. COLETTI. *Catalogo delle cose d'arte e di antichità della Provincia di Treviso,* Rome, 1935.

L. COLETTI. "La crisi manieristica nella pittura veneziana," in *Convivium,* 1941.

L. COLETTI. *Tutta la pittura di Giorgione,* Milan, 1955.

W. G. CONSTABLE. "Dipinti di raccolte inglesi alla mostra d'arte italiana a Londra," in *Dedalo,* 1929–30.

H. COOK. *Giorgione,* London, 1900.

H. COOK. "The Date of Birth of Titian," in *The Nineteenth Century,* 1900.

H. COOK. "When Was Titian Born?", in *Rep. für Kunstwissenschaft,* 1902.

H. COOK. "Did Titian Live to be Ninety-nine Years Old?", in *The Nineteenth Century,* 1902.

H. COOK. "Three Unpublished Italian Portraits," in *The Burlington Magazine,* 1903.

H. COOK. "The Identification of Two Painters' Portraits," in *The Burlington Magazine,* 1904–05.

H. COOK. "The True Portrait of Laura de' Dianti by Titian", in *The Burlington Magazine,* 1905.

H. COOK. "Notes on the Study of Titian," in *The Burlington Magazine,* 1906.

H. COOK. *Reviews and Appreciation*, London, 1912.

H. COOK. *The portrait of Caterina Cornaro by Giorgione (finished by Titian)*, London, 1915.

H. COOK. "Recensione al *Giorgione* dello Justi," in *The Burlington Magazine*, 1926.

M. L. COX. "Inventory of the Arundel Collection," in *The Burlington Magazine*, 1911.

L. CURTIUS. "Zum Antikenstudium Tizians," in *Archiv für Kulturgeschichte*, 1933.

L. CUST. *The Chatsworth Van Dyck Sketchbook*, London, 1902.

L. CUST. "'The Lovers' by Titian," in *The Burlington Magazine*, 1916.

L. CUST. "Titian at Hampton Court," in *Apollo*, 1928.

P. D'ANCONA and L. GENGARO. *Umanesimo e Rinascimento* (3rd ed.), Milan, 1953.

C. D'ARCO. *Delle Arti e degli artefici di Mantova . . .*, Mantua, 1857.

G. DE BATZ. *Giorgione and His Circle*, Baltimore, 1942.

M. DE BENEDETTI. "Una 'Sacra famiglia' giovanile di Tiziano," in *Emporium*, 1950.

C. DE BROSSES. *Lettres d'Italie*, Dijon, 1739.

H. DEBRUNNER. "A Masterpiece by Lorenzo Lotto," in *The Burlington Magazine*, 1928.

E. DELACROIX. *Journal*, 3 vols., Paris, 1893.

G. A. DELL'ACQUA. *Tiziano*, Milan, 1955.

P. DELLA PERGOLA. *Giorgione*, Milan, 1955.

P. DELLA PERGOLA. *Cataloghi dei Musei e delle Gallerie d'Italia—Galleria Borghese, I dipinti*, Vol. I, Rome, 1955.

A. DELLA ROVERE. "Tiziano Vecellio: le sue Madonne addolorate," in *Arte e Storia*, 1902.

G. DE LOGU. *Tiziano*, Bergamo, 1934.

G. DE LOGU. *L'amor sacro e profano*, Milan, 1947.

G. DE LOGU. *Tiziano*, Bergamo, 1951.

P. H. DE MINERBI. "Gli affreschi al Fondaco dei Tedeschi," in *Bollettino d'Arte*, 1936–37.

P. H. DE MINERBI. *La "Tempesta" di Giorgione e "L'Amor Sacro e Profano" di Tiziano nello spirito umanista di Venezia*, Milan, 1939.

J. DEWNISTOUN. *Memoirs of the Dukes of Urbino*, London, 1909.

N. DI CARPEGNA. *Catalogo della Galleria Nazionale—Palazzo Barberini*, Roma, 1953.

L. DOLCE. *Dialogo della pittura . . . intitolato l'Aretino*, Venice, 1557.

F. DULBERG. *Tizian*, Leipzig, 1924.

L. DUSSLER. "Tizian-Austellung in Venedig," in *Zeitschrift für Kunstgeschichte*, 1935.

M. DVORAK. *Italienische Kunst*, Vol. II, Munich, 1928.

P. EGAN. "Poesia and the Fête Champêtre," in *The Art Bulletin*, 1959.

M. VON EINEM. *Karl V und Tizian*. Cologne, 1960.

E. VON ENGERTH. *Kunsthistorisches Sammlungen des Allerhöchsten Kaiserhauses-gemälde*, Vienna, 1882.

G. EVANS. "Notes on Titian's 'Venus and The Luteplayer'," in *The Art Bulletin*, 1947.

C. FABBRO. "Un ritratto inedito di Tiziano," in *Arte Veneta*, 1952.

C. FABBRO. "La casa natale di Tiziano a Pieve di Cadore. Cenni storici," in *Archivio storico di Belluno, Feltre e Cadore,* 1953.

C. FABBRO. "Documenti editi ed inediti su Tiziano e sulla famiglia Vecellio, conservati nella casa di Tiziano a Pieve di Cadore," in *Archivio storico di Belluno, Feltre e Cadore,* 1953.

C. FABBRO. "Documenti su Tiziano e sulla famiglia Vecellio conservati nella casa di Tiziano a Pieve di Cadore," in *Archivio Storico di Belluno, Feltre e Pieve di Cadore,* 1956.

A. FELIBIEN. *Entretiens sur les vies et sur les ouvrages des plus excellens peintres anciens et modernes,* Paris, 1668–88, and Amsterdam, 1705.

G. FIOCCO. "An Historical Titian," in *The Burlington Magazine,* 1924.

G. FIOCCO. "Piccoli maestri: La Pittura bresciana del Cinquecento a Padova," in *Bollettino d'Arte,* 1927.

G. FIOCCO. *Giovanni Antonio Pordenone,* Udine, 1939.

G. FIOCCO. *Giorgione,* Bergamo, 1941.

G. FIOCCO. *Un Tiziano: la "Venere delle Colombe,"* Venice, 1942.

G. FIOCCO. "Francesco Vecellio," in *Lettere ed Arti,* 1946.

G. FIOCCO. "Un Tiziano dimenticato," in *Arte Veneta,* 1947.

G. FIOCCO. "Tiziano o Paolo Veronese," in *Arte Veneta,* 1948.

G. FIOCCO. *Giorgione,* Bergamo, 1948 (2nd ed.).

G. FIOCCO. Introduction, in F. Valcanover and C. Fabbri, *Catalogo della Mostra dei Vecellio,* Belluno, 1951.

G. FIOCCO. "La Mostra dei Vecellio a Belluno," in *Emporium,* 1951.

G. FIOCCO. "Il ritratto di Sperone Speroni dipinto da Tiziano," in *Bollettino d'Arte,* 1954.

G. FIOCCO. "Profilo di Francesco Vecellio," I, in *Arte Veneta,* 1955.

G. FIOCCO. "Profilo di Francesco Vecellio," II, in *Arte Veneta,* 1955.

G. FIOCCO. "A Small Portable Panel by Titian for Philip II," in *The Burlington Magazine,* 1956.

G. FIOCCO. "Profilo di Francesco Vecellio," III, in *Arte Veneta,* 1956.

G. FIOCCO. "Un Tiziano ricuperato," in *Arte Veneta,* 1957.

G. FIOCCO. "Ancora del ritratto di Sperone Speroni di Tiziano," in *Bollettino d'Arte,* 1957.

G. FIOCCO. *La civiltà veneziana del Rinascimento: le arti figurative,* Florence, 1958.

G. FIOCCO. "La 'Crocifissione' di Tiziano all'Escuriale e Orazio Vecellio," in *Studies in the History of Art Dedicated to William Suida,* London, 1959.

O. FISCHEL. "Tizian" (*Klassiker der Kunst*), Stuttgart, 1904, and editions up to 1929.

O. FISCHEL. "Der Mädchenkopf aus Tizians Schlacht von Cadore," in *Kunstkronik,* 1921–22.

O. FISCHEL. "Two Unknown Portraits of Titian," in *Art in America,* 1925–26.

G. FOGOLARI. "Artisti lombardi del primo Cinquecento che operarono nelle Venezie: Francesco da Milano," in *Rassegna d'Arte,* 1914.

G. FOGOLARI. "La 'Venere' di Dresda è quella di Giorgione in Casa Marcello?" in *L'Ateneo Veneto,* 1933–34.

G. FOGOLARI. *Mostra di Tiziano,* Catalog, Venice, 1935.

A. FORATTI. "Tiziano nella Scuola del Santo," in *Cronache d'Arte,* 1928.

L. FOSCARI. *Iconografia di Tiziano,* Venice, 1935.

D. FREY. "Tizian und Michelangelo, zum Problem des Manierismus," in *Museion Studien aus Kunst u. Geschichte für O.H. Förster*, Cologne, 1960.

W. FRIEDLÄNDER. "La Tintura delle rose," in *The Art Bulletin*, 1938.

F. FRIMMEL. *Blätter für Gemäldekunde*, Supplement V, 1909.

G. FRIZZONI. Edition of the manuscript in the Biblioteca Marciana by M. A. Michiel (cf. M. A. Michiel, below), Bologna, 1884.

G. FRIZZONI. "Serie di capolavori dell'arte italiana nuovamente illustrati," in *Archivio Storico dell'Arte*, 1892.

G. FRIZZONI. "Nuove rivelazioni intorno a Iacopo Palma il Vecchio," in *Rassegna d'Arte*, 1906.

L. FRÖHLICH-BUM. "Andrea Meldolla genannt Schiavone," in *Jahrbuch der Sammlungen des a.h. Kaiserhauses*, 1913.

L. FRÖHLICH-BUM. "Five Drawings for Titian's Altarpiece of St. Peter Martyr," in *The Burlington Magazine*, 1924.

L. FRÖHLICH-BUM. "Studien zu Handzeichnungen der italienischen Renaissance," in *Jahrbuch der Kunsthistorischen Sammlungen in Wien*, 1928.

R. FRY. "The Bridgewater Titians," in *The Burlington Magazine*, 1933.

R. FRY and A. G. B. RUSSELL. "Tizian's Ariosto," in *The Burlington Magazine*, 1904–05.

P. FUCHS. "La coperta con 'l'impresa d'amore' dipinta da Tiziano pel ritratto di Sperone Speroni," in *Dedalo*, 1928–29.

R. GALLO. "Per il 'Lorenzo Martire,' di Tiziano," in *Rivista di Venezia*, 1935.

C. GAMBA. "La 'Venere' di Giorgione reintegrata," in *Dedalo*, 1928–29.

C. GAMBA. *Tiziano*, Novara, 1941.

C. GAMBA. "Il mio Giorgione," in *Arte Veneta*, 1954.

G. GAMULIN. "Tizianov poliptik u Katedrali u Dubrovniku," in *Zborrik Institute za historijske nanke Zadru*, 1955.

G. GAMULIN. "Un polittico del Tiziano nella Cattedrale di Ragusa," in *Venezia e l'Europa*, 1956.

G. GAMULIN. "Un quadro di Tiziano troppo dimenticato," in *Commentari*, 1957.

A. GARDIN. *Errori di G.B. Cavalcaselle e G.A. Crowe nella storia . . . della pala di Tiziano a Castel Roganzuolo*, Florence, 1883.

G. GAYE. *Carteggio inedito d'artisti*, Florence, 1840.

G. GEROLA. "Il supposto ritratto del Fracastoro dipinto da Tiziano," in *Archivio storico veneto*, 1910.

O. V. GERSTFELD. "Venus und Violante," in *Monatsheft für Kunstwissenschaft*, 1910.

C. GILBERT. "Sante Zago e la cultura artistica del tempo," in *Arte Veneta*, 1952.

J. GILBERT. *Cadore, or Titian's Country*, London, 1869.

G. GIOMO. "S. Pietro Martire e Tiziano," in *Nuovo archivio veneto*, 1903.

D. GIOSEFFI. *Tiziano*, Bergamo, 1959.

G. GLUCK. "Bildnisse aus dem Hause Habsburg—I. Kaiserin Isabella," in *Jahrbuch der Kunsthistorischen Sammlungen*, 1933.

G. GLUCK. "Bildnisse aus dem Hause Habsburg—II. Konigin Maria von Ungarn," in *Jahrbuch der Kunsthistorischen Sammlungen*, 1934.

U. GNOLI. "Amor sacro e profano," in *Rassegna d'arte*, 1902.

G. GOMBOSI. "Tizians Bildnis der Victoria Farnese," in *Jahrbuch der preussischen Kunstsammlungen*, 1928.

G. GOMBOSI. "Il ritratto di Filippo II del Tiziano nella Galleria Corsini," in *Bollettino d'Arte*, 1928–29.

G. GOMBOSI. *Palma Vecchio*, Stuttgart-Berlin, 1937.

G. GOMBOSI. "Über venezianischen Bildnisse," in *Pantheon*, 1937.

D. GONZATI. *La Basilica di Sant'Antonio da Padova*, Padua, 1852–53.

S. J GORE. "An Ecce Homo in Dublin," in *The Burlington Magazine*, 1955.

S. J. GORE. "Five Portraits," in *The Burlington Magazine*, 1958.

C. GOULD. "A Famous Titian Restored," in *The Burlington Magazine*, 1958.

C. GOULD. *National Gallery Catalogue. The Sixteenth-Century Venetian School*, London, 1959.

G. GRAPPE. *Titien*, Paris, 1942.

L. GRASSI. *Tiziano*, Rome, 1945.

E. GRAZZINI COCCO. "Pittori cinquecenteschi padovani," in *Bollettino del Museo Civico di Padova*, 1927.

G. GRONAU. "Tizians Geburtsjahr," in *Rep. für Kunstwissenschaft*, 1900.

G. GRONAU. *Tizian*, Berlin, 1900 (English edition, London, 1904).

G. GRONAU. "Tizian als Porträtmaler," in *Das Museum*, 1900.

G. GRONAU. "Tiziano Bildnis der Moritz von Sachsen," in *Rep. für Kunstwissenschaft*, 1900.

G. GRONAU. "Titians Bildnisse türkischer Sultaninnen," in *Beiträge zur Kunstgeschichte, F. Wickoff gewidmet*, Vienna, 1903.

G. GRONAU. "Tizians 'Himmlische und irdische Liebe'," in *Rep. für Kunstwissenschaft*, 1903.

G. GRONAU. "Titian's Portrait of the Empress Isabella," in *The Burlington Magazine*, 1903.

G. GRONAU. "Die Kunstbestebungen der Herzoge von Urbino," in *Jahrbuch der preuss. Kunstsammlungen*, 1904 and 1906.

G. GRONAU. "Titians Bildnis des Pietro Aretino in London," in *Zeitschrift für Bildende Kunst*, 1905.

G. GRONAU. "Il ritratto di Giovanni dalle Bande Nere attribuito a Tiziano," in *Rivista d'arte*, 1905.

G. GRONAU. "Zwei tizianische Bildnisse der Berliner Galerien," in *Jahrbuch der preuss. Kunstsammlungen*, 1906.

G. GRONAU. "Tizians Selbstbildnis der Berliner Galerie," in *Jahrbuch der preuss. Kunstsammlungen*, 1907.

G. GRONAU. "Di due quadri di Tiziano poco conosciuti," in *Rassegna d'arte*, 1907.

G. GRONAU. "Kritische Studien zu Giorgione," in *Rep. für Kunstwissenschaft*, 1908.

G. GRONAU. "Die Cäsarenbilder von Tiziano," in *Münchner Jahrbuch der Bildenden Kunst*, 1908.

G. GRONAU. "Giorgione," in *Thieme-Becker Kunstlerlexikon*, Vol. XIV, Leipzig, 1921.

G. GRONAU. "Über einige unbekannte Bildnisse von Tizian," in *Zeitschrift für Bildenden Kunst*, 1922.

G. GRONAU. "Concerning Titian's Pictures at Alnwick Castle," in *Apollo*, 1925.

G. GRONAU. "The 'Fracastoro' Portrait in the Mond Collection," in *The Burlington Magazine*, 1926.

G. GRONAU. "Tizian und Alfonso d'Este," in *Jahrbuch der Kunsthistorisches Sammlungen in Wien*, 1928.

G. GRONAU. "Tizian" (*Klassiker der Kunst*), Stuttgart, 1930.

G. GRONAU. "Tizians 'Ariosto'," in *The Burlington Magazine*, 1933.

G. GRONAU. "Un ritratto del duca Guidobaldo d'Urbino dipinto da Tiziano," in *Miscellanea di Storia dell'Arte in onore di I. B. Supino*, Florence, 1933.

G. GRONAU. *Documenti artistici urbinati*, Florence, 1936.

G. GRONAU. "Alcuni quadri di Tiziano illustrati da documenti," in *Bollettino d'Arte*, 1936–37.

G. GRONAU. "Bemerkungen zur jüngsten Tizian-Forschung," in *Belvedere*, 1937.

G. GRONAU. "Some Portraits by Titian and Raphael," in *Art in America*, 1937.

E. GROSE. "Notes on Titian's 'Venus and the Luteplayer'," in *The Art Bulletin*, 1947.

L. GROSSATO. *Il Museo Civico di Padova*, Catalog, Venice, 1957.

N. A. GURVIC. *Titian*, Leningrad, 1940 (in Russian).

G. HABICH. "Die Imperatoren-Bilder in der Münchener Residenz," in *Monatsheft für Kunstwissenschaft*, 1908.

M. HAMEL. *Titien*, Paris, 1903.

G. F. HARTLAUB. "Étude sur un tableau du Titien," in *Arte*, 1937.

G. F. HARTLAUB. "Antike Wahrsagungsmotive in Bildern Tizians," in *Pantheon*, 1941.

G. F. HARTLAUB. "Tizians 'Liebesorakel' und seine 'Kristallseherin'. Ein Beitrag zur weltlichen Ikonographie der Renaissance," in *Zeitschrift für Kunst*, 1950.

F. HEINEMANN. *Tizian: Die Zwei ersten Jahrzehnte seiner künstlerischen Entwicklung*, Munich, 1928.

P. HENDY. "Titian at Hertford House," in *The Burlington Magazine*, 1925.

P. HENDY. "Ein berühmter Tizian wieder aufgetaucht," in *Pantheon*, 1933.

P. HENDY. "More about Giorgione's 'Daniel and Susannah' at Glasgow," in *Arte Veneta*, 1954.

F. HERMANIN. "Zur Wiederöffnung der Gemäldegalerie in Palazzo Spada," in *Pantheon*, 1931.

F. HERMANIN. *Il mito di Giorgione*, Spoleto, 1933.

T. HETZER. "Tizian und Carpaccio," in *Monatsheft für Kunstwissenschaft*, 1914.

T. HETZER. *Die frühen Gemälde Tizians*, Basel, 1920.

T. HETZER. "Studien über Tizians Stil," in *Jahrbuch fur Kunstwissenschaft*, 1923.

T. HETZER. *Tizian, Geschichte seiner Farbe*, Frankfurt, 1935.

T. HETZER. "Vecellio, Tiziano," in *Thieme-Becker Künstlerlexikon*, Vol. XXXIV, Leipzig, 1940.

T. HETZER. *Tizian*, Frankfurt, 1948.

P. HOFER. "Die Pardo-Venus Tizians," in *Festschrift Hans F. Hahnloser*, Basilea-Stoccarda. 1962.

C. HOLMES. "'La Schiavona' by Titian," in *The Burlington Magazine*, 1914–15.

C. HOLMES. "Titian's 'Venus and Adonis' in the National Gallery," in *The Burlington Magazine*, 1924.

C. HOLMES. "A Preparatory Version of Titian's 'Trinity'," in *The Burlington Magazine*, 1924.

C. HOLMES. "The Inscription Upon Titian's Portrait of Franceschi," in *The Burlington Magazine*, 1929.

J. G. HOOGEWERFF. "Un bozzetto di Tiziano per la pala dei Pesaro," in *Bollettino d'arte*, 1927–28.

L. HOURTICQ. "La 'Fontaine d'amour' de Titien," in *Gazette des Beaux-Arts*, 1917.

L. HOURTICQ. *La Jeunesse de Titien*, Paris, 1919.

L. HOURTICQ. *Le problème de Giorgione*, Paris, 1930.

A. HUME. *Notices on the Life and Works of Titian*, London, 1829.

R. HUYGHE. *Le Titien*, Paris, 1949.

F. INGERSOLL SMOUSE. "A propos de trois tableaux du Titien," in *Gazette des Beaux-Arts*, 1923.

F. INGERSOLL SMOUSE. "Une œuvre de la vieillesse du Titien: 'Lucrèce et Tarquin' et ses deux répliques," in *Gazette des Beaux-Arts*, 1926.

E. JACOBSEN. "Études du Titien pour les 'Bacchanales' de Londres et Madrid," in *Gazette des Beaux-Arts*, 1908.

S. JAREMITCH. "Le Portrait du V. Cappello par le Titien," in *Annuaire du Musée de l'Ermitage*, 1936.

G. JEDLICKA. "Über einige Spätwerke von Tizian," in *Werk*, 1947.

K. JUHNIG. *Tizien*, Munich, 1921.

C. JUSTI. "Verzeichnis der frührer in Spanien befindlichen jetz verschollen oder in Ausland gekomenen Gemälde Tizians," in *Jahrbuch der preuss. Kunstsammlungen*, 1889.

C. JUSTI. "Tizian und Alfonso d'Este," in *Jahrbuch der preuss. Kunstsammlungen*, 1894.

C. JUSTI. "Das Tizianbildnis der Königlichen Galerie zu Kassel," in *Jahrbuch der preuss. Kunstsammlungen*, 1894.

C. JUSTI. "Die Bildnisse der Kardinale Hyppolit von Medici in Florenz," in *Zeitschrift für Bildende Kunst*, 1897.

C. JUSTI. "Laura Dianti," in *Jahrbuch der preuss. Kunstsammlungen*, 1899.

C. JUSTI. "Tizian und der Hof von Urbino," in *Jahrbuch der preuss. Kunstsammlungen*, 1904.

C. JUSTI. *Miscell. aus drei Jahrhundert span. Kunstlebens*, 1908.

C. JUSTI. *Giorgione*, Berlin, 1908, and editions of 1926 and 1936.

R. W. KENNEDY. *Novelty and tradition in Titian's art*, Northampton, Mass., 1963.

S. KENNEDY NORTH. "Titian's 'Venus' at Bridgewater House," in *The Burlington Magazine*, 1932.

H. KNACKFUSS. *Tizian*, Bielefeld-Leipzig, 1903, passim.

W. KORN. *Tizians Holzschnitte*, Breslau, 1897.

F. KREYCZI. "Urkunden und Regesten aus dem Kaiserlichen und Königslichen Reichs-Finz-Archiv," in *Jahrbuch der Sammlungen des a.h. Kaiserhauses*, V, 2, 1887.

P. KRISTELLER. *Il Trionfo della Fede*, Berlin, 1906.

P. KRISTELLER. "Tizians Beziehungen zum Kupferstich," in *Mitteilungen der Gesellschaft für vervielfältingende Kunst*, 1911.

B. KURTH. "Ein verschollenes Gemälde Tizians," in *Die Graphische Künste*, 1938.

G. LAFENESTRE. *La vie et l'œuvre de Titien*, Paris, 1886 (2nd ed., 1909).

G. LAFENESTRE. "Les dernières années de Titien," in *L'artiste*, 1886.

G. LAFENESTRE. "Les portraits des Madruzzi, par Titien et G. B. Moroni," in *Revue de l'Art ancien et moderne*, 1907.

R. LANGTON DOUGLAS. "The Date of Titian's Birth," in *The Art Quarterly*, 1948.

O. LANZ. "Ein Tizian-Porträt in Holland," in *Belvedere*, 1922.

L. LANZI. *Storia pittorica d'Italia*, Bassano, 1789.

J. LAUTS. "Venetian Painting in the 16th Century and its European Resonance," in *Venezia e l'Europa, Atti del XVIII Congresso Internazionale di Storia dell'Arte*, Venice, 1956.

A. LAZZARI. "Il ritratto del Mosti di Tiziano," in *Arte Veneta*, 1952.

H. LEPORINI. *Tizian*, Vienna-Leipzig, 1925.

C. LOESER. *Disegni di Tiziano Vecellio e di Jacopo Robusti*, Florence, 1912.

G. P. LOMAZZO. *Trattato dell'arte della Pittura*, Milan, 1584.

G. P. LOMAZZO. *Idea del tempio della Pittura*, Milan, 1590.

R. LONGHI. "Piero dei Franceschi e lo sviluppo della pittura veneziana," in *L'Arte*, 1914.

R. LONGHI. "Giunte a Tiziano," in *L'Arte*, 1925.

R. LONGHI. "Cartella tizianesca," in *Vita artistica*, 1927.

R. LONGHI. *Precisazioni nelle Gallerie italiane: la Galleria Borghese*, Rome, 1928.

R. LONGHI. *Officina ferrarese*, Rome, 1934.

R. LONGHI. *Viatico per cinque secoli di pittura veneziana*, Florence, 1946.

R. LONGHI. "Calepino veneziano: XI.—Tiziano e 'l'Ostensione delle Santissime Croci' a Brescia," in *Arte Veneta*, 1947.

R. LONGHI. "Una citazione tizianesca nel Caravaggio," in *Arte Veneta*, 1954.

R. LONGHI. *Officina ferrarese*, Florence, 1956.

M. LORENTE JUNQUERA. "La 'Santa Margarita' de Tiziano en el Escorial," in *Archivo Español de Arte*, 1951.

M. LORENTE JUNQUERA. "Il ritratto del Connestabile di Borbone di Tiziano," in *Arte Veneta*, 1953.

G. LORENZETTI. "Per la storia del 'Cristo portacroce' della Chiesa di San Rocco a Venezia," in *Venezia*, 1920.

G. LORENZETTI. *Venezia e il suo estuario*, Rome, 1926 (2nd edition, 1956).

G. B. LORENZI. *Monumenti per servire alla storia del Palazzo Ducale di Venezia*, Venice, 1868, passim.

A. LORENZONI. *Cadore*, Bergamo, 1907.

O. LUDWIG. "Die Hochzeit Tizians," in *Jahrbuch der preuss. Kunstsammlungen*, 1903.

O. LUDWIG. "Archivalische Beiträge zur Geschichte der venetianischen Kunst," in *Italienische Forschungen, herausgegeben vom Kunsthistorischen Institut in Florenz*, IV. Band, Berlin, 1911.

A. LUZIO. *L'Aretino e la corte dei Gonzaga*, Turin, 1884.

A. LUZIO. "Tre lettere di Tiziano al Card. Ercole Gonzaga," in *Archivio Storico dell'Arte*, 1890.

A. LUZIO. "I ritratti di Isabella d'Este," in *Emporium*, 1900.

A. LUZIO. *La Galleria dei Gonzaga*, Milan, 1913.

A. LUZIO. "Le Maddalene di Tiziano," in *La lettura*, 1940.

A. LUZIO-RENIER. *Mantova e Urbino*, Turin, 1895.

B. MALFATTI and T. GAR. "Lettera di G. della Torre a Cristoforo Madruzzo," in *Calendario Trentino per l'anno 1874*.

G. C. MALVASIA. *Felsina pittrice*, Bologna, 1678.

F. MANIAGO. *Storia delle belle arti friulane,* Udine, 1823.
A. MARANGONI. *Come si guarda un quadro,* Florence, 1927.
H. MARCEAU. "Titian's 'Virgin and Child with St. Dorothy'," in *The Philadelphia Museum Bulletin,* 1957.
A. MARTINI. "Spigolature venete," in *Arte Veneta,* 1957.
F. J. MATHER. "An Enigmatic Venetian Picture," in *The Art Bulletin,* 1927.
F. J. MATHER. "When Was Titian Born?", in *The Art Bulletin,* 1938.
F. J. MATHER, JR. "Titian Problem: The Seven Acts of Mercy," in *Gazette des Beaux-Arts,* 1942.
E. MAUCERI. "Bologna, Regia Pinacoteca: Restauro di una 'Crocifissione' di Tiziano," in *Bollettino d'Arte,* 1931.
C. MAUCLAIR. *Le Titien,* Paris, 1925.
F. MAURONER. *Le incisioni di Tiziano,* Venice, 1941 (2nd ed., 1943).
A. L. MAYER. "Zwei unbekannte Gemälde aus Tizian Spätzeit," in *Belvedere,* 1924.
A. L. MAYER. "Tizianstudien," in *Münchner Jahrbuch der Bild Kunstenden,* 1925.
A. L. MAYER. "An Unknown Portrait of Titian's Middle Period," in *Apollo,* 1926.
A. L. MAYER. "A Newly Discovered Masterpiece by Titian," in *Apollo,* 1927.
A. L. MAYER. "Eine 'Anbetung der heiligen drei Könige' von Tizian," in *Pantheon,* 1930.
A. L. MAYER. "Nachrichten—London," in *Pantheon,* 1930.
A. L. MAYER. "Versteigerung der Sammlung von Heyl," in *Pantheon,* 1930.
A. L. MAYER. "The Yarborough 'Magdalen' by Titian," in *Apollo,* 1930.
A. L. MAYER. "Zur Giorgione-Tizian-Frage," in *Pantheon,* 1932.
A. L. MAYER. "Una ignorata 'Madre dolorosa' di Tiziano," in *L'Arte,* 1935.
A. L. MAYER. "An Unknown 'Ecce Homo' by Titian," in *The Burlington Magazine,* 1935.
A. L. MAYER. "Two Pictures by Titian in the Escorial," in *The Burlington Magazine,* 1937.
A. L. MAYER. "A propos d'un nouveau livre sur le Titien," in *Gazette des Beaux-Arts,* 1937.
A. L. MAYER. "Quelques notes sur l'œuvre de Titien," in *Gazette des Beaux-Arts,* 1938.
A. L. MAYER. "Beiträge zu Tizian," in *Critica d'Arte,* 1938.
A. L. MAYER. "Aurelio Nicolò: The Commissioner of Titian's 'Sacred and Profane Love'," in *The Art Bulletin,* 1939.
R. B. K. MCLANATHAN. "Dipinti veneziani acquistati negli ultimi anni dal Museo di Belle Arti di Boston," in *Arte Veneta,* 1950.
A. R. MENGS. *Opere,* Bassano, 1783.
E. V. MEYER. *Die Seele Tizians zur Psychologie der Renaissance,* Esslingen, 1900.
M. A. MICHIEL (ANONIMO MORELLIANO). *Notizie d'opere di disegno (1521–1543),* Ms. in the Biblioteca Marciana: ed. Morelli, Bassano, 1800; ed. Frizzoni, Bologna, 1884.
H. MILES. *Titian,* London, 1906.
I. MILICUA. "A proposito del pequeño Crucifijo Ticianesco del Escorial," in *Archivio Español de Arte,* 1957.
P. MOLMENTI. "Le nozze di Tiziano Vecellio," in *Atti del Regio Instituto di Scienze, Lettere ed Arti,* 1904.

F. MONOD. "La Galerie Altman au Metropolitan Museum de New-York," in *Gazette des Beaux-Arts, 1923.*

A. MORASSI. *Giorgione,* Milan, 1942.

A. MORASSI. "Il Tiziano in casa Balbi," in *Emporium,* 1946.

A. MORASSI. "Esordi di Tiziano," in *Arte Veneta,* 1954.

A. MORASSI. *Tiziano. Gli affreschi della Scuola del Santo a Padova,* Milan, 1956.

A. MORASSI. "Ritratti del periodo giovanile di Tiziano," in *Festschrift für W. Sas-Zaloziecky zum 60. Geburtstag,* Graz, 1956.

A. MORASSI. *Tiziano,* Milan, 1964.

A. MORASSI. "Tiziano," in *Enciclopedia Universale dell'Arte,* 1964.

G. MORELLI (J. LERMOLIEFF). *Die Werke italienischer Meister in den Galerien von München, Dresden und Berlin,* Leipzig, 1880 (Italian ed., Bologna, 1886).

G. MORELLI (J. LERMOLIEFF). *Kunstkritische Studien über italienische Malerei. Die Galerien Borghese und Doria Panfili in Rom,* Leipzig, 1890–93.

I. MORELLI. Edition of the manuscript in the Biblioteca Marciana by M. A. Michiel (see below under M. A. Michiel), Bassano, 1800.

J. MORENO VILLA. "Como son y como eran unos Tizianos del Prado," in *Archivio Español de Arte y Arqueología,* 1933.

B. MORSOLIN. "Opere di Tiziano ignorate o perdute," in *Arte e Storia,* 1890.

B. MORSOLIN. "Tiziano a Vicenza," in *Arte e Storia,* 1892.

A. MOSCHETTI. *I danni artistici nelle Venezie nella guerra mondiale 1915–18,* Venice, 1932.

M. MURARO. "Due nuovi Lorenzo Lotto fra i musaici di San Marco," in *Arte Veneta,* 1948.

M. MURARO. "Il memoriale di Zuan Paolo da Ponte," in *Archivio Veneto,* 1949.

A. NEOUSTROIEFF. "The Italian Pictures in the Collection of Duke G.N. von Leuchtenberg of Petrograd," in *L'Arte,* 1903.

J. NEUMANN. *Titian, the Flaying of Marsyas,* London, 1962.

E. NEWTON. "Round the National Gallery, 10. 'Bacchus and Ariadne', by Titian, 1480?–1576," in *Art News and Review,* 1957.

G. NICCO FASOLA. "Il Manierismo e L'Arte veneziana del Cinquecento," in *Venezia e l'Europa, Atti del XVIII Congresso Internazionale di Storia dell'Arte,* Venice, 1956.

C. NORDENFALK. "Tizians Darstellung des Schauens," in *Nationalmusei Arsbok,* 1947–48 (published in 1950).

C. NORDENFALK. "Titian's Allegories on the Fondaco dei Tedeschi," in *Gazette des Beaux-Arts,* 1952.

C. NORRIS. "Tizians Exhibition," in *The Burlington Magazine,* 1935.

L. OBERZINER. "Il ritratto di Cristoforo Madruzzo di Tiziano," in *Strenna per l'Alto Adige,* Trent, 1900.

K. OETTINGER. "Tizians Verkündigung in Treviso," in *Münchner Jahrbuch,* 1930.

K. OETTINGER. "Giorgione und Tiziano am Fondaco dei Tedeschi," in *Belvedere,* 1932.

K. OETTINGER. "Die wahre Giorgione-Venus," in *Jahrbuch des Kunsthistorischen Sammlungen in Wien,* 1944.

U. OJETTI. "Tiziano e il Cadore," in *Rivista di Venezia,* 1932.

S. ORTOLANI. "Restauro d'un Tiziano," in *Bollettino d'Arte,* 1948.

L. OZZOLA. "Venere ed Elena," in *L'Arte,* 1906.

L. OZZOLA. "Un presunto ritratto di Tiziano," in *Bollettino d'Arte, 1931*.
L. OZZOLA. "Il 'San Pietro' di Tiziano al Museo di Anversa e la sua data," in *Bollettino d'Arte, 1932–33*.
L. OZZOLA. *Studi su Tiziano,* Strasbourg, 1939.
G. and Z. PAGELLO. *Memorie e documenti intorno ai dipinti di Tiziano Vecellio nella chiesa arcidiaconale di Pieve di Cadore,* Nozze Monti-Segato, Belluno, 1900.
R. PALLUCCHINI. "La Mostra di Tiziano," in *Ateneo Veneto, 1935.*
R. PALLUCCHINI. Review of *Tizian* by H. L. Tietze, in *L'Arte, 1937.*
R. PALLUCCHINI. *Sebastian Viniziano,* Milan, 1944.
R. PALLUCCHINI. *I dipinti della Galleria Estense di Modena,* Roma, 1945.
R. PALLUCCHINI. *I Capolavori dei Musei Veneti,* Exhibition Catalog, Venice, 1946.
R. PALLUCCHINI. "Opere di Tiziano e del Tintoretto acquistate da Musei Americani," in *Arte Veneta, 1950.*
R. PALLUCCHINI. *La giovinezza del Tintoretto,* Milan, 1950.
R. PALLUCCHINI. "Una mostra di pittura veneziana a Londra," in *Arte Veneta, 1953.*
R. PALLUCCHINI. *Tiziano* (Lectures given at the Fine Arts Faculty of the University of Bologna during the years 1952–54), Vol. II, Bologna, 1953–54 (with bibliography).
R. PALLUCCHINI. *Giorgione,* Milan, 1955.
R. PALLUCCHINI. "Guida alla Mostra del Giorgione," in *Le Arti, 1955.*
R. PALLUCCHINI. "La Mostra del Centenario a Manchester," in *Arte Veneta, 1957.*
R. PALLUCCHINI. "Un nuova ritratto di Tiziano," in *Arte Veneta, 1958.*
R. PALLUCCHINI. "Contributi alla pittura veneta del Cinquecento: 'El Cristo morto' Vendramin," in *Arte Veneta, 1959–60.*
R. PALLUCCHINI. "Studi tizianeschi," in *Arte Veneta, 1961.*
I. M. PALMARINI. "'Amor Sacro e Profano' e 'La fonte di Ardenna'," in *Nuova Antologia, 1902.*
A. PALOMBO Y VELASCO. *El Museo Pictorico,* Madrid, 1715–24.
E. PANOFSKY. "Hercules am Scheidewege. Excurs I: Zur Deutung von Tizians 'Himmlischer und irdischer Liebe'," *Studien der Bibliotek Warburg herausgegeben von Fritz Saxl,* XVIII, Leipzig-Berlin, 1930.
K. T. PARKER. "La 'Cena in Emmaus' di Tiziano a Brocklesby Park," in *Arte Veneta, 1952.*
C. PEEZ. *Tizians Schmerzenreiche Madonnen,* Vienna, 1912.
La peinture vénitienne (Catalog of the Exhibition of Venetian Painting), Amsterdam, 1953.
G. PERATÉ, in A. MICHIEL, *Histoire de l'Art,* Vol. IV, Paris, 1909.
M. PERKINS. "An Unpublished Painting by Titian," in *Art in America, 1921.*
C. PHILLIPS. *The Earlier Work of Titian,* London, 1897.
C. PHILLIPS. *The Later Work of Titian,* London, 1898.
C. PHILLIPS. *Titian: a Study of His Life and Works,* London, 1898.
C. PHILLIPS. "The 'Perseus and Andromeda' of Titian," in *The Nineteenth Century,* 1900.
C. PHILLIPS. "The Titian of the Cassel Gallery," in *The Burlington Magazine,* 1912.
D. PHILLIPS. *The Leadership of Giorgione,* Washington, 1937.

T. PIGNATTI. *Giorgione,* Milan, 1955.

A. PINCHART. "Tableaux et Sculptures de Charles-Quint," *in Revue Universelle des Arts,* 1856.

A. PINCHART. "Tableaux et Sculptures de Marie d'Autriche," in *Revue Universelle des Arts,* 1856.

P. PINO. *Dialogo di Pittura,* Venice, 1548. (R. and A. Pallucchini's edition: Venice, 1946.)

M. PITTALUGA. "Un Tiziano di meno," in *Dedalo,* 1933.

S. POGLAYEN NEUWALL. "Tizianstudien," in *Münchner Jahrbuch für Bildende Kunst,* 1927.

S. POGLAYEN NEUWALL. "Ein wiederaufgetauchtes Früwerk Tiziano?", in *Der Cicerone,* 1927.

S. POGLAYEN NEUWALL. "Eine tizianische 'Toilette der Venus' aus dem Cranach-Kreis im Zusammenhang mit verwandten Darstellungen Titians und deren Kopien," in *Münchner Jahrbuch für Bildende Kunst,* 1929.

S. POGLAYEN NEUWALL. "Titian's Pictures of the 'Toilet of Venus' and Their Copies," in *The Bulletin of the College Art Association,* Chicago, 1934.

S. POGLAYEN NEUWALL. "The 'Venus of the Ca' d'Oro' and the Origin of the Chief Types of the 'Venus and the Mirror' from the Workshops of Titian," in *The Art Bulletin,* 1947.

A. POPE. *Titian's "Rape of Europa,"* London, 1962.

A. E. POPP. "Tizians 'Lukrezia und Tarquin'," in *Zeitschrift für Bildende Kunst,* 1921.

A. PORCELLA. *Le pitture della Galleria Spada,* Rome, 1931.

H. POSSE. "Die Rekonstruktion der 'Venus mit Cupido' von Giorgione," in *Jahrbuch der preussischen Kunstsammlungen,* 1931.

L. PUNGILEONI. "Notizie spettanti a Tiziano Vecellio di Cadore," in *Nuovo Archivio Veneto,* 1920.

C. L. RAGGHIANTI, in Vasari, *Le Vite . . .,* Milan, 1942–43.

A. RAPP. "Zuschreibung an Tizian," in *Die Weltkunst,* 1957.

A. RAVA. "Il 'Camerino delle Anticaglie' di Gabriele Vendramin," in *Nuovo Archivio Veneto,* 1920.

J. REYNOLDS. *Works,* London, 1798.

C. RICCI. "Ritratti tizianeschi di Gian Paolo Pase," in *Rivista del Regio Istituto di Archeologia ed Historia d'Arte,* 1929.

G. M. RICHTER. "Two Titian Self-Portraits," in *The Burlington Magazine,* 1931.

G. M. RICHTER. "Titian's 'Venus and the Lute Player'," in *The Burlington Magazine,* 1931.

G. M. RICHTER. "The Three Different Types of Titian's Self-Portraits," in *Apollo,* 1931.

G. M. RICHTER. "A Clue to Giorgione's Late Style," in *The Burlington Magazine,* 1932.

G. M. RICHTER. "The Bridgewater Titian," in *Apollo,* 1933.

G. M. RICHTER. "The problem of 'Noli me Tangere'," in *The Burlington Magazine,* 1934.

G. M. RICHTER. *Giorgio da Castelfranco, called Giorgione,* Chicago, 1937.

G. M. RICHTER. "Giorgione's evolution . . ." in: De Batz, *Giorgione and his circle,* Baltimore, 1942.

G. M. RICHTER. "Lost and Rediscovered Works by Giorgione," in *Art in America,* 1942.

J. P. RICHTER. *Italian Art in the National Gallery,* London, 1883.

C. RICKETTS. *Titian,* London, 1910.

C. RIDOLFI. *Le maraviglie dell'arte della pittura,* Venice, 1648 (ed. Von Hadeln, Berlin, 1914 and 1924).

H. RIEGEL. "Tizians Gemälde der 'Himmlischen und irdischen Liebe'," in *Beiträge zur Kunstgeschichte Italiens,* Dresden, 1898.

H. RIEGEL. "Die Gemälde der 'Danaë' von Correggio und Tizian," in *Beiträge zur Kunstgeschichte Italiens,* Dresden, 1898.

H. RIEGEL. "Tizians Bildnisse der Herzogin Eleonora Gonzaga von Urbino," in *Beiträge zur Kunstgeschichte Italiens,* Dresden, 1908.

E. RIGONI. *Appunti e documenti sul pittore Girolamo del Santo,* Padua, 1941.

F. RINTELEN. "Tizians portrait des Antonio Anselmi," in *Jahrbuch der preuss. Kunstsammlungen,* 1905.

G. ROBERTSON. "The Giorgione Exhibition in Venice," in *The Burlington Magazine,* 1955.

A. RONCHINI. "Delle relazioni di Tiziano coi Farnese," in *Atti e Memorie delle Regie Deputazioni di Storia Patria per le Provincie modenesi e parmensi,* 1864.

G. B. ROSSETTI. *Descrizione . . . di Padova . . . di G. B. Rossetti,* Padua, 1780.

E. VON ROTHSCHILD. "Tizians Darstellungen des Laurentiusmarter," in *Belvedere,* 1931.

T. ROUSSEAU. *Tizian,* New York, 1955.

H. RUHEMANN. "The Cleaning and Restoration of the Glasgow Giorgione," in *The Burlington Magazine,* 1955.

A. SAGARIZZI. "Una lotteria di quadri nel secolo XVIII," in *Nuovo Archivio Veneto,* 1914.

A. SALAZAR and F. I. SANCHÉZ CANTON. *Retratos del Museo del Prado,* Madrid, 1919.

A. SALAZAR and F. I. SANCHÉZ CANTON. *Museo del Prado, Catalogo de los cuadros,* Madrid, 1949.

R. SALVINI. *Galleria degli Uffizi,* Novara, 1954.

F. SANSOVINO. *Venezia, Città nobilissima,* Venice, 1581; 2nd ed. "corrected, amended, and . . . expanded" by S. Stringa, Venice, 1604; 3rd ed. "with additions" by G. Martinioni, Venice, 1663.

M. SANUDO. *I Diari (1496–1533),* Venice, 1879–1903.

F. SCANNELLI. *Il microcosmo della Pittura,* Cesena, 1657.

L. SCARAMUCCIA. *Le finezze dei pennelli italiani,* Pavia, 1674.

E. SCHAEFFER. "Noch einmal das Bildnis des Vincenzo Cappello," in *Monatsheft für Kunstwissenschaft,* 1909.

E. SCHAEFFER. "Ein Bildnis des Hieronymus Fracostoro von Tiziano," in *Jahrbuch der preuss. Kunstsammlungen,* 1910.

A. SCHARF. "Rubens's Portraits of Charles V and Isabella," in *The Burlington Magazine,* 1935.

W. SCHMIDT. "Zur Kenntnis Giorgiones," in *Rep. für Kunstwissenschaft,* 1908.

D. VON SCHONHERR. "Urkunden und Regesten aus dem Kaiserlichen und Königslichen Staathalterei-Archiv in Innsbruck," in *Jahrbuch der Sammlungen des a.h. Kaiserhauses,* II, 2, 1884; XI, 2, 1890.

P. SCHUBRING. "A surmise concerning the subject of the Venetian figure painting in the Detroit Museum," in *Art in America*, 1927.

P. SELVATICO. *Storia estetico-critica delle arti del disegno*, Venice, 1856.

P. SELVATICO. *Di alcuni abbozzi di Tiziano . . . nella Galleria Giustinian Barbarigo in Padova*, Padua, 1875.

S. SINDING-LARSEN. "Titian's Madonna di Les Pezaro and its historical significance" in Acta ad. archaeologiens et artium historiam pertinentia 1. Oslo, 1962.

O. SIRÉN. *Dessins et tableaux de la Renaissance italienne dans les collections de Suède*, Stockholm, 1902.

G. SOLIMENE. *Un umanista veneziano* (Bartolomeo Morante) *giudica Tiziano*, Naples, 1953.

A. SPAHN. *Palma il vecchio*, Leipzig, 1932.

S. SPERONI. *Dialogo d'amore*, Venice, 1542.

J. STARZYNSKI. "Quelques réflexions sur le réalisme dans l'art du Titien," in *Venezia e l'Europa, Atti del XVIII Congresso Internazionale di Storia dell'Arte*, Venice, 1956.

A. STIX. "Tizians 'Diana und Kalliste'," in *Jahrbuch der Sammlungen des a.h. Kaiserhauses*, 1913.

G. STRINGA. See: F. SANSOVINO. *Venetia, Città nobilissima*, 2nd ed., Venice, 1604.

W. G. STUDDERT-KENNEDY. "Titian: The Fitzwilliam Venus," in *The Burlington Magazine*, London, 1958.

W. SUIDA. "Unbekannte Bildnisse von Tizian," in *Belvedere*, 1922.

W. SUIDA. "Rivendicazioni a Tiziano," in *Vita artistica*, 1927.

W. SUIDA. "Tizians Bildnis des Mons. D'Aramont," in *Belvedere*, 1929.

W. SUIDA. "Un second 'Homme au gant' de Titien au Louvre," in *Gazette des Beaux-Arts*, 1930.

W. SUIDA. "Alcune opere sconosciute di Tiziano," in *Dedalo*, 1930–31.

W. SUIDA. "Zum Werke des Palma Vecchio," in *Belvedere*, 1931.

W. SUIDA. "Tizians 'Kind mit Taube'," in *Belvedere*, 1932.

W. SUIDA. *Tiziano*, Rome, 1933 (German edition, Zürich, 1933; French edition, Paris, 1935).

W. SUIDA. "New Light on Titian's Portrait," in *The Burlington Magazine*, 1934.

W. SUIDA. "Titians frühestes Danaëbild," in *Belvedere*, 1934–35.

W. SUIDA. "Einige Bildnisse von Tizian," in *Belvedere*, 1934–35.

W. SUIDA. "Tizian, die beide Campagnola und Ugo da Carpi," in *La critica d'arte*, 1936.

W. SUIDA. "Titian's Earliest Portrait of 'Aretino'," in *The Burlington Magazine*, 1939.

W. SUIDA. "Forgotten Splendor in Titian's Treasures," in *Art in America*, 1941.

W. SUIDA. "Addenda to Titian's Religious Oeuvre," in *Gazette des Beaux-Arts*, 1943.

W. SUIDA. "Titian's Portraits, Original and Reconstructions," in *Gazette des Beaux-Arts*, 1946.

W. SUIDA. "Miscellanea tizianesca," I, in *Arte Veneta*, 1952.

W. SUIDA. *The Samuel H. Kress Collection—M. H. De Young Memorial Museum*, San Francisco, 1955.

W. SUIDA. "Miscellanea tizianesca," II, in *Arte Veneta*, 1956.

w. suida. "Miscellanea tizianesca," III, in *Arte Veneta,* 1957.

R. R. tatlock. "An Uncatalogued Titian," in *The Burlington Magazine,* 1925.

R. R. tatlock. "An Unpublished Titian," in *Apollo,* 1934.

E. tea. "La 'Pala Pesaro', e 'l'Immacolata'," in *Ecclesia,* 1958.

D. teniers. *Antverpiensis Pictoris et Cubiculis Serenissimis Principus . . .* (*Theatrum Pictorium*), Brussels-Antwerp, 1660.

C. terrasse. *Titien,* Paris, 1930.

G. de tervarent. "Les deux Amours. A propos d'un tableau de Titien à la Galerie Borghèse à Rome," in *Bulletin de l'Institut Historique Belge de Rome,* Brussels, 1963.

M. thausing. "Tizian und die Herzogin Eleonora von Urbino," in *Zeitschrift für Bildende Kunst,* 1878.

H. thode. *Tintoretto,* Leipzig, 1901.

S. ticozzi. *Vite dei pittori Vecelli di Cadore,* Milan, 1817.

E. tietze-conrat. "Zu Titians 'Schlacht bei Cadore'," in *Die Grafische Kunst,* 1925.

E. tietze-conrat. "A Rediscovered Early Masterpiece by Titian ('Rest on Flight into Egypt,' Leningrad, Hermitage)," in *Art in America,* 1941.

E. tietze-conrat. "Neglected Contemporary Sources Relating to Michelangelo and Titian," in *The Art Bulletin,* 1943.

E. tietze-conrat. "The 'Holkham Venus' in the Metropolitan Museum," in *The Art Bulletin,* 1944.

E. tietze-conrat. "Titian as a Letter Writer," in *The Art Bulletin,* 1944.

E. tietze-conrat. "Titian's 'Battle of Cadore,'" in *The Art Bulletin,* 1944.

E. tietze-conrat. "The So-called 'Adulteress' by Giorgione," in *Gazette des Beaux-Arts,* 1945.

E. tietze-conrat. "The 'Wemyss Allegory' in the Art Institute of Chicago," in *The Art Bulletin,* 1945.

E. tietze-conrat. "Titian's Workshop in His Late Years," in *The Art Bulletin,* 1946.

E. tietze-conrat. "Titian's Portrait of Paul III," in *Gazette des Beaux-Arts,* 1946.

E. tietze-conrat. "Titian's Design for the 'Battle of Cadore'," in *Gazette des Beaux-Arts,* 1948.

E. tietze-conrat. "Das Skizzenbuch des Van Dyck als Quelle für die Tizianforschung," in *La critica d'arte,* 1950.

E. tietze-conrat. "La xilografia di Tiziano 'Il Passaggio del Mar Rosso'," in *Arte Veneta,* 1950.

E. tietze-conrat. "Titian's 'Allegory of Religion'," in *Journal of the Warburg and Courtauld Institutes,* 1951.

E. tietze-conrat. "The 'Pesaro Madonna,' a Footnote on Titian," in *Gazette des Beaux-Arts,* 1953.

E. tietze-conrat. "Un soffitto di Tiziano a Brescia conservato in un disegno del Rubens," in *Arte Veneta,* 1954.

E. tietze-conrat. "Titian's 'Saint Catherine'," in *Gazette des Beaux-Arts,* 1954.

E. tietze-conrat. "'L'Adorazione dei Magi' di Tiziano dipinta per il Cardinale di Ferrara," in *Emporium,* 1954.

E. tietze-conrat. "Titian as a Landscape Painter," in *Gazette des Beaux-Arts,* 1955.

E. TIETZE-CONRAT. "Archeologia tizianesca," in *Arte Veneta*, 1956.

H. TIETZE. *Tizian, Leben und Werk*, 2 vols., Vienna, 1936.

H. TIETZE. "The 'Faun and Nymph' in the Boymans Museum in Rotterdam," in *The Art Quarterly*, 1939.

H. TIETZE. "A drawing by Titian," in *Art in America*, 1943.

H. TIETZE. "Unknown Venetian Renaissance drawing in Swedish Collection," in *Gazette des Beaux-Arts*, 1949.

H. TIETZE. *Titian. Paintings and Drawings*, London, 1950 (also in German and French; revised edition of the monograph published in 1936).

H. TIETZE. "An early version of Titian's 'Danae'. An Analysis of Titian's replicas," in *Arte Veneta*, 1954.

H. TIETZE and E. TIETZE-CONRAT. "Tizian-Studien," in *Jahrbuch der Kunsthistorischen Sammlungen in Wien*, 1930.

H. TIETZE and E. TIETZE-CONRAT. "Tizian-Graphik," in *Die Graphische Kunst*, 1938.

H. TIETZE and E. TIETZE-CONRAT. "Titian's Woodcuts," in *The Print Collector's Quarterly*, 1938.

H. TIETZE and E. TIETZE-CONRAT. "On several drawings erroneously attributed to Titian," in *Gazette des Beaux-Arts*, 1942.

H. TIETZE and E. TIETZE-CONRAT. *The Drawings of the Venetian Painters of the XV and XVI Centuries*, New York, 1944.

H. TIETZE and E. TIETZE-CONRAT. "I ritratti Spilimbergo a Washington," in *Emporium*, 1953.

K. TSCHEUSCHNER. "Über den Tizian n. 172 der Dresdner Galerie," in *Repertorium*, 1901.

O. ULM. "I ritratti di Irene ed Emilia di Spilimbergo erroneamente attribuiti a Tiziano," in *Emporium*, 1910.

G. URBANI. "Ricupero di un Tiziano ('Le stimmate di San Francesco,' Museo Provinciale di Ascoli Piceno)," in *Bollettino dell'Istituto Centrale del Restauro*, 1951.

G. URBANI. "Schede di restauro. Tiziano: 'La Vergine che appare a S. Francesco, S. Biagio e un committente,' Ancona, Chiesa di S. Domenico," in *Bollettino dell'Istituto Centrale del Restauro*, 1952.

G. URBANI. "Schede di restauro. Tiziano: 'Le stimmate di S. Francesco,' Trapani, Museo Civico," in *Bollettino dell'Istituto Centrale del Restauro*, 1954.

F. VALCANOVER. *Catalogo della mostra del Vecellio*, Belluno, 1951.

F. VALCANOVER. "La Mostra dei Vecellio a Belluno," in *Arte Veneta*, 1951.

F. VALCANOVER. "Il polittico vecelliano di Sedico," in *Archivio Storico di Belluno, Feltre e Cadore*, 1955.

W. R. VALENTINER. "'Toilette de Venus-Goldman'," in *Belvedere*, 1922.

W. R. VALENTINER. "A Combined Work by Titian, Giorgione and Sebastiano del Piombo," in *Detroit Bulletin*, 1926.

W. R. VALENTINER. *Unknown Masterpieces in Public and Private Collections*, London, 1930.

W. R. VALENTINER. "Ein Alteswerk Tizians," in *Pantheon*, 1935.

M. VALSECCHI. *La pittura veneziana*, Milan, 1954.

M. VALSECCHI. *Tiziano*, Milan, 1958.

G. VASARI. *Le vite de' più eccellenti architetti, pittori et scultori italiani*, 1st ed., Florence, 1550; 2nd ed., Florence, 1568 (published in G. Milanesi's edition, Florence, 1881; in C. L. Ragghianti's edition, Milan, 1942–43).

C. VECELLIO. *Degli Habiti Antichi e Moderni . . .,* Venice, 1590. *De Venetiaanse Meesters* (Catalog of the Exhibition of Venetian Painting), Amsterdam, 1953; and later catalogs of Brussels (1953) and Paris (1954).
A. VENTURI. *Il Museo della Galleria Borghese,* Rome, 1893.
A. VENTURI. *La Galleria Crespi,* Milan, 1900.
A. VENTURI. "Per Tiziano," in *L'Arte,* 1926.
A. VENTURI. "Un'opera dimenticata di Tiziano a Napoli," in *L'Arte,* 1926.
A. VENTURI. *Storia dell'arte italiana. La pittura del Cinquecento,* Part VII, Vol. II, Milan, 1926; Part IX, Vol. III, Milan, 1928.
A. VENTURI. "Tiziano nel Cadore," in *Vita artistica,* 1927.
A. VENTURI. "Quadro ignoto di Tiziano," in *L'Arte,* 1927.
A. VENTURI. "Doppio ritratto di Tiziano," in *L'Arte,* 1932.
A. VENTURI. "Tre ritratti inediti di Tiziano," in *L'Arte,* 1937.
A. VENTURI. "'Ecce Homo' di Tiziano a Budapest," in *L'Arte,* 1940.
L. VENTURI. "Saggio sulle opere d'arte italiana a Pietroburgo," in *L'Arte,* 1912.
L. VENTURI. *Giorgione e il giorgionismo,* Milan, 1913.
L. VENTURI. *Pitture italiane in America,* Milan, 1931.
L. VENTURI. "Contributi a Tiziano," in *L'Arte,* 1932.
L. VENTURI. *Italian Paintings in America,* Milan, 1933.
L. VENTURI. "Tre pitture venete della Collezione Rabinowitz," in *Arte Veneta,* 1947.
L. VENTURI. *La Peinture Italienne—La Renaissance,* Genoa, Paris, New York, 1951.
L. VENTURI. *Giorgione,* Rome, 1954.
L. VENTURI. *Titian,* New York, 1954.
L. VENTURI. "L'Ultimo Tiziano," in *Epoche Maestri della pittura italiana.* Turin, 1956.
F. VERGERIO. *La chiesa monumentale di Santa Maria di Lentiai* (extract), Alassio, 1931.
L. VERTOVA. *Tiziano,* Florence, 1951.
F. VILLOT. *Notice des tableaux du Musée du Louvre,* Paris, 1852.
D. VON HADELN. "Zu Tizian in Padua," in *Rep. für Kunstwissenschaft,* 1908.
D. VON HADELN. "Zum datum der 'Bella' Tizians," in *Rep. für Kunstwissenschaft,* 1909.
D. VON HADELN. "Bildnis des Dogen Niccolò Marcello in der Pinakothek des Vaticano," in *Rep. für Kunstwissenschaft,* 1910.
D. VON HADELN. "Über Zeichnungen der fürheren Zeit Tizians," in *Jahrbuch der preuss. Kunstsammlungen,* 1913.
D. VON HADELN. Edition of *Ridolfi,* Berlin, 1914.
D. VON HADELN. *Tiziano Handzeichnungen,* Berlin, 1924.
D. VON HADELN. "Some little known Works of Titian," in *The Burlington Magazine,* 1924.
D. VON HADELN. "Another version of the 'Danae' by Titian," in *The Burlington Magazine,* 1926.
D. VON HADELN. "Two drawings by Titian," in *Art in America,* 1927.
D. VON HADELN. "Two unknown works by Titian," in *The Burlington Magazine,* 1928.
D. VON HADELN. "Ein Gruppenbildnis von Tizian," in *Pantheon,* 1929.
D. VON HADELN. "Dogenbildnisse von Tizian," in *Pantheon,* 1930.

D. VON HADELN. "Das Problem der Lavinia-Bildnisse," in *Pantheon,* 1931.

D. VON HADELN. "The 'Venus with the Lute Player' by Titian," in *Pantheon,* 1932.

D. VON HADELN. "Tizians Bildnis des Giovanni Francesco Acquaviva," in *Pantheon,* 1934.

H. VON VOLTELLINI. "Urkunden und Regesten aus dem Kaiserlichen u. Königlichen Haus-Hof-und-Staats-Archiv. in Wien," in *Jahrbuch der Sammlungen des a.h. Kaiserhauses,* XI, 2, 1890; XIII, 2, 1892.

H. VOSS. "Rembrandt und Tizian," in *Rep. für Kunstwissenschaft,* 1905.

G. F. WAAGEN. *Künstwerke und Künstler in England und Paris,* Berlin, 1839.

G. F. WAAGEN. *Treasures of Art in Great Britain,* London, 1854 and 1857.

E. WALDMANN. "Zur frage von Tizians Geburts," in *Jahrbuch Kunstchronik,* 1921.

E. WALDMANN. *Tizian,* Berlin, 1922.

J. WALKER. *Bellini and Tizian at Ferrara. A Study of Styles and Taste,* London, 1956.

E. K. WATERHOUSE. *Titian's "Diana and Actaeon,"* Oxford, 1952.

H. B. WEHLE. *A Catalog of Italian, Spanish and Byzantine Paintings,* The Metropolitan Museum, New York, 1940.

F. WICKHOFF. "Les écoles italiennes au Musée impérial de Vienne," in *Gazette des Beaux-Arts,* 1893.

F. WICKHOFF. "Giorgiones Bilder zu römischen Heldegedichten," in *Jahrbuch der preuss. Kunstsammlungen,* 1895.

F. WICKHOFF. "Die 'Andrier des Philostrat' von Tizian," in *Jahrbuch der preuss. Kunstsammlungen,* 1902.

F. WICKHOFF. Review of the monographs by Gronau and Fischel, in *Kunstgeschichtliche Anzeigen,* 1904.

F. WICKHOFF. Review of: Ludwig Justi, *Giorgione,* in *Kunstgeschichtliche Anzeigen,* 1909.

R. WIEGMAN. *Die malweise des Tizian,* Düsseldorf, 1847.

K. WILCZEK. "Tizians 'Emmauswunder' in Louvre," in *Jahrbuch der preuss. Kunstsammlungen,* 1928.

K. WILCZEK. "Ein Bildnis des A. d'Avalos, Tizian," in *Zeitschrift für Bildende Kunst,* 1929–30.

J. WILDE. "Wiedergefundene Gemälde aus der Sammlung des Erzherzogs Leopold Wilhelm," in *Jahrbuch der Kunsthistorischen Sammlungen in Wien,* 1930.

J. WILDE. "Die Probleme um Dominico Mancini," in *Jahrbuch der Kunsthistorischen Sammlungen in Wien,* 1933.

J. WILDE. "Zwei Tizian-Zuschreibungen des 17. Jahrhunderts," in *Jahrbuch der Kunsthistorischen Sammlungen in Wien,* 1934.

R. WIND. *Bellini's "Feast of the Gods,"* Cambridge, Mass., 1948.

E. WIND. "A note on 'Bacchus and Ariadne'," in *The Burlington Magazine,* 1950.

R. B. WISCHITZER. "New Interpretation of Titian's 'Sacred and Profane Love'," in *Gazette des Beaux-Arts,* 1943.

R. WITTKOWER. "Les écoles italiennes au Musée Impérial de Vienne," in *Gazette des Beaux-Arts,* 1893.

R. WITTKOWER and M. MACLAREN. "Titian's Allegory of 'Religion Succoured by Spain'," in *Journal of the Warburg and Courtauld Institute,* 1939–40.

H. WOELFFLIN. *Die Klassische Kunst,* Munich, 1899 (translated into Italian, Florence, 1941).

O. WULFF. "Tizians Kolorit in seiner Enfaltung und Nachwirkung," in *Zeitschrift für Aesthetik u. allgemeine Kunstwissenschaft,* 1937.

O. WULFF. "Farbe, Licht und Schatten in Tizian Bildgestaltung. Die lehren der Mostra di Tiziano von 1935," in *Jahrbuch der preuss. Kunstsammlung n,* 1941.

I. ZABARELLA and I. CARENIA. *Aule Zabarella . . . ,* Padua, 1670.

B. ZAMBONI. *Memorie intorno alle pubbliche fabbriche più insigni della città di Brescia,* Brescia, 1778.

P. ZAMPETTI. *Giorgione e i giorgioneschi* (Catalog of the Exhibition), Venice, 1955.

P. ZAMPETTI. "Postille alla Mostra di Giorgione," in *Arte Veneta,* 1955.

G. B. ZANDONELLA. *Elogio di Tiziano Vecellio,* Venice, 1802.

A. M. ZANETTI. *Varie pitture a fresco de' principali Maestri Veneziani . . . ,* 1760.

A. M. ZANETTI. *Della pittura veneziana e delle opere pubbliche de' veneziani maestri,* Venice, 1771.

F. ZANOTTO. *Nuovissima Guida di Venezia . . . ,* Venice, 1856.

M. R. ZARCO DEL VALLE. "Unveröffentlichte Beiträge zur Geschichte der Kunstbestrebungen Karles V. und Philipp II.," in *Jahrbuch der Sammlungen des a.h. Kaiserhauses,* VII, 1888.

J. ZARNOWSKY. "Una composizione smarrita di Tiziano," in *Rivista d'arte,* 1935.

J. ZARNOWSKI. "L'atelier de Titien: Girolamo Dente," in *Dawna Sztuka,* 1938.

E. ZIMMERMANN. *Die Landschaft in der Venetianischen Malerei,* Leipzig, 1893.

H. ZIMMERMANN. "Zur richtigen Datierung eine Porträts von Tizian in den Wiener K. Gemälde-Galerie," in *Mitteilungen des Instituts für Oesterreichische Geschichtforschung Ergänzungsband,* VI.

H. ZINNEMANN. "Das Inventar der Prager Schatz und Kunstkammern von 6 Dez. 1621," in *Jahrbuch der Kunsthistorischen Sammlungen des a.h. Kaiserhauses,* XXV, Part 2, 1905.

REPRODUCTIONS

ACKNOWLEDGMENT
FOR PLATES

Plates 1, 10, 20, 22, 25, 30, 31, 32, 33, 35, 37, 43, 44, 45, 47a, 48, 53, 55, 57, 58, 65, 70, 71, 74, 75, 77, 78, 79, 104a, 105, 110, 111, 113, 114, 115, 116, 118, 119, 127, 128, 129, 130, 131, 148b, 162b, 168, 179: *Anderson, Rome*. Plates 2, 96, 156a and b, 192; *Alinari, Florence*. Plates 3, 6, 7, 12, 38, 64, 72, 80, 81, 102, 103, 106, 107, 108, 112, 122, 123, 132, 133, 135, 149, 155a, 164b, 182: *Fiorentini, Venice*. Plates 13, 36, 66, 67, 68, 69, 125, 144, 159, 175: *Rossi, Venice*. Plates 100, 101: Istituto Centrale del Restauro, Rome. Plate 146: *A.F.I., Venice*. Plate 184: *Brogi, Florence*. Plate 185: *Gabinetto Fotografico Nazionale, Rome*. Plates 186a and b, 187a and b, 188, 189, 190, 191, 195, 197b, 198: reproduced from engravings. The remaining black and white plates were provided by the galleries and collections to which the pictures belong. Material for Color Plate I (Part 3) was supplied by Scala, Florence. Material for the other color plates in Parts 3 and 4 was supplied by the Prado Museum, Madrid.

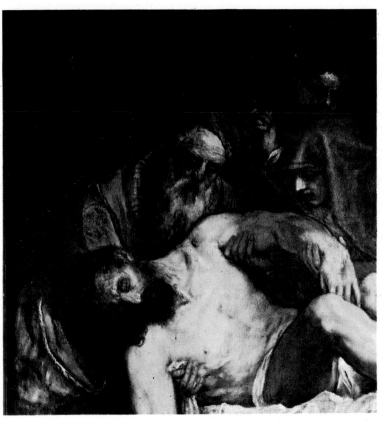

THE ENTOMBMENT, Madrid, Prado
(*detail of plate 79*)

Plate 112. ST MARY MAGDALENE
Leningrad, Hermitage

Plate 113. ST MARGARET AND THE DRAGON
Madrid, Prado

Plate 114. VENUS BLINDFOLDING CUPID
Rome, Borghese Gallery

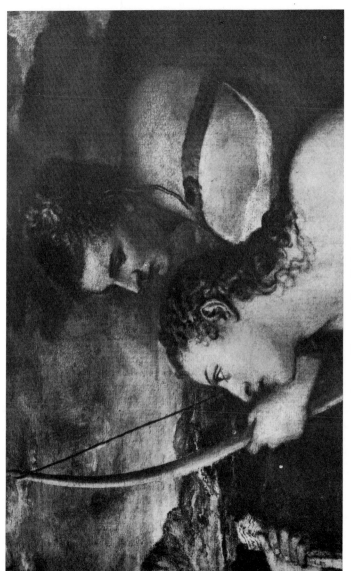

Plate 115. *Detail of plate 114*

Plate 116. *Detail of plate 114*

Plate 117. JUDITH
Detroit, Institute of Arts

Plate 118. ST DOMINIC
Rome, Borghese Gallery

Plate 119. CHRIST AT THE COLUMN
Rome, Borghese Gallery

Plate 120. ALLEGORY OF PRUDENCE
London, private collection

Plate 121. THE MARTYRDOM OF ST LAWRENCE
Escorial, Monastery of St Lawrence

Plate 122. PORTRAIT OF JACOPO STRADA
Vienna, Kunsthistorisches Museum

Plate 123. *Detail of plate 122*

Plate 124. THE ENTOMBMENT
Madrid, Prado

Plate 125. MADONNA AND CHILD BETWEEN SS TITIAN AND ANDREW
Pieve di Cadore, Archdiaconate

Plate 126. THE TRIBUTE MONEY
London, National Gallery

SELF-PORTRAIT, Madrid, Prado

Plate 127. CHRIST CARRYING THE CROSS
Madrid, Prado

Plate 128. SELF-PORTRAIT
Madrid, Prado

Plate 129. THE FALL OF MAN
Madrid, Prado

Plate 130. SPAIN COMING TO THE AID OF RELIGION
Madrid, Prado

Plate 131. PHILIP II OFFERING THE INFANTE DON FERNANDO TO
VICTORY
Madrid, Prado

Plate 132. ST SEBASTIAN
Leningrad, Hermitage

Plate 133. *Detail of plate 132*

Plate 134. THE CROWN OF THORNS
Munich, Bayerische Staatsgemäldesammlungen

Plate 135. ECCE HOMO
St. Louis, Art Museum

Plate 136. TARQUIN AND LUCRETIA
Cambridge, Fitzwilliam Museum

Plate 137. TARQUIN AND LUCRETIA
Vienna, Gemäldegalerie der Akademie der Bildenden Kunst

Plate 138. *Detail of plate 137*

Plate 139. MADONNA AND CHILD
London, National Gallery

Plate 140. CHILD WITH DOGS
Rotterdam, Boymans Museum

Plate 141. NYMPH AND SHEPHERD
Vienna, Kunsthistorisches Museum

Plate 142. *Detail of plate 141*

THE FALL OF MAN, Madrid, Prado
(*detail of plate 129*)

Plate 143. THE PUNISHMENT OF MARSYAS
Kromieriz, National Gallery

Plate 144. THE DEPOSITION
Venice, Accademia

Plate 145. *Detail of plate 144*

Plate 146. *Detail of plate 144*

ATTRIBUTED PAINTINGS

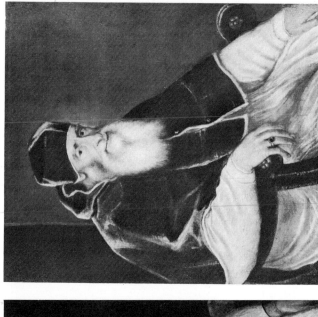

Plate 147. PORTRAIT OF POPE PAUL III
Leningrad, Hermitage, *and* Vienna, Kunsthistorisches Museum (*both attrib.*)

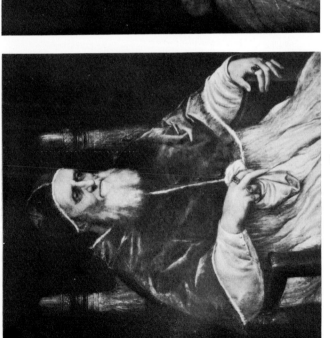

Plate 148. PORTRAIT OF POPE JULIUS II
Florence, Pitti Palace
and PORTRAIT OF CARDINAL ALESSANDRO FARNESE
Tivoli, Villa d'Este (both attrib.)

Plate 149. SUPPOSED PORTRAIT OF VITTORIA FARNESE
Budapest, Museum of Fine Arts (*attrib.*)

Plate 150. PORTRAIT OF A MAN IN FURS
São Paulo, Museum of Art (*attrib.*)

Plate 151. THE EDUCATION OF LOVE
New York, Kress Collection (*attrib.*)

Plate 152. DANAË
New York, Hickox Collection (*attrib.*)

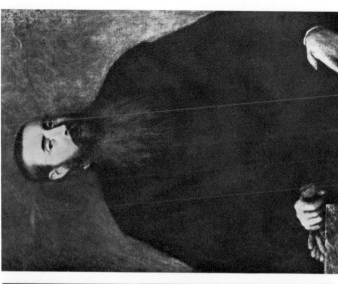

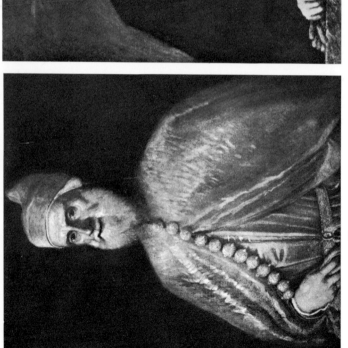

Plate 153. PORTRAIT OF THE DOGE FRANCESCO DONATO
San Diego, Fine Arts Gallery
and PORTRAIT OF A MAN WITH GLOVES
Munich, Bohler Collection (*both attrib.*)

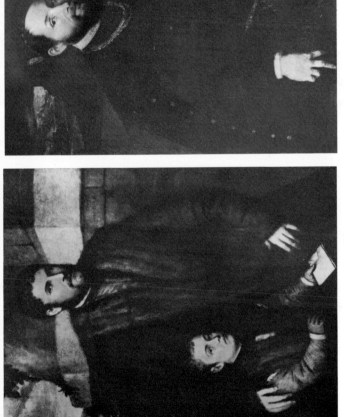

Plate 154. DOUBLE PORTRAIT
Padua, private collection
and PORTRAIT OF A VENETIAN NOBLEMAN
New York, Metropolitan Museum, Bache Collection (*both attrib.*)

Plate 155. SUPPOSED PORTRAIT OF FERDINAND I
Naples, Capodimonte
and PORTRAIT OF ANDREA DE' FRANCESCHI
Indianapolis, Clowes Collection (*both attrib.*)

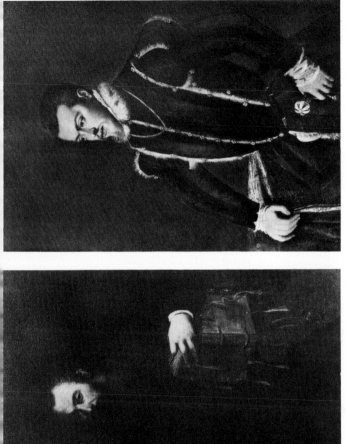

Plate 156. SUPPOSED PORTRAIT OF ANDREA VESALIO
Florence, Pitti Palace
and PORTRAIT OF PHILIP II
Rome, Barberini Palace (*both attrib.*)

Plate 157. PORTRAIT OF THE DUKE OF ACQUAVIVA
Lucerne, Bohler Collection (*attrib.*)

SPAIN COMING TO THE AID OF RELIGION
(*detail of plate 130*)

Plate 158. CHRIST BETWEEN TWO EXECUTIONERS
Paris, Louvre (*attrib.*)

Plate 159. TRIPTYCH
Castello Roganzuolo (Ceneda), Parish Church (*attrib.*).

Plate 160. POLYPTYCH
Dubrovnik, Cathedral (*attrib.*)

Plate 161. MARY MAGDALENE, WITH ST BIAGO, TOBIAS, THE ANGEL,
AND THE DONOR
Dubrovnik, Church of St Dominic
and CRUCIFIXION
Madrid, Royal Palace *(both details)*

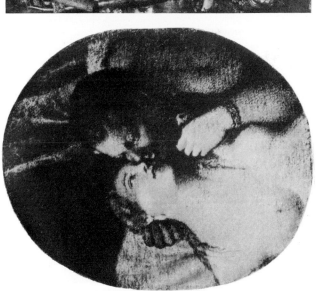

Plate 162. JOVE AND ANTIOPE
Munich, Bayerische Staatsgemäldesammlungen
and VENUS AND ADONIS
Rome, Barberini Palace (*both attrib.*)

Plate 163. NYMPH AND FAUN
Rotterdam, Boymans Museum
and PORTRAIT OF A MAN WITH BOOK
Copenhagen, Statens Museum for Kunst *(both attrib.)*

Plate 164. SUPPOSED PORTRAIT OF FILIPPO STROZZI
Vienna, Kunsthistorisches Museum
and PORTRAIT OF A BEARDED MAN
Copenhagen, Statens Museum for Kunst (*both attrib.*)

Plate 165. PORTRAIT OF A NOBLEWOMAN
Washington, National Gallery of Art (*attrib.*)

Plate 166. PORTRAIT OF THE DOGE MARCANTONIO TREVISAN
Budapest, Museum of Fine Arts (*attrib*.)

Plate 167. PORTRAIT OF A MONK

Bowood (Calne, Wilts), Collection of the Marquis of Lansdowne
and ECCE HOMO

Dublin, National Gallery of Ireland *(both attrib.)*

Plate 168. CHRIST AND SIMON OF CYRENE
Madrid, Prado (*attrib.*)

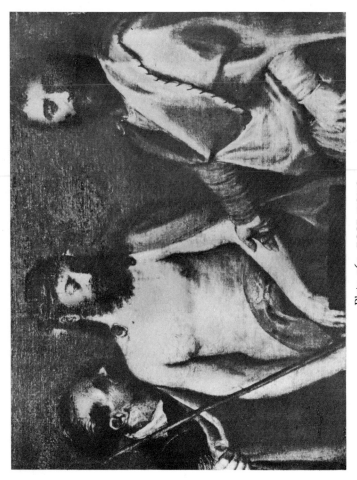

Plate 169. ECCE HOMO
Escorial, Monastery of St Lawrence (*attrib.*)

Plate 170. THE ADORATION OF THE MAGI
Aarburg, Löthy Collection (*attrib.*)

Plate 171. THE ADORATION OF THE MAGI
Cleveland, Museum of Art (*attrib.*)

Plate 172. THE ADORATION OF THE MAGI
Madrid, Prado (*attrib.*)

Plate 173. MADONNA AND CHILD
Rome, Albertini Collection (*attrib.*)

Plate 174. PORTRAIT OF ARCHBISHOP FILIPPO ARCHINTO
New York, Metropolitan Museum (*attrib.*)

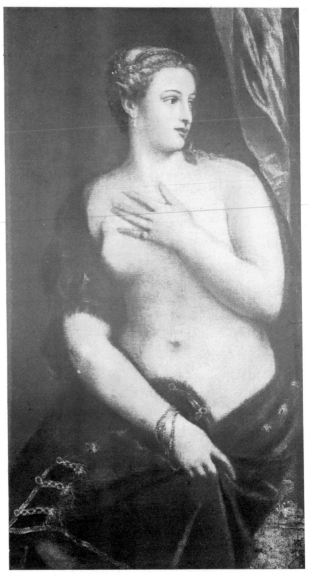

Plate 175. VENUS
Venice, Galleria Franchetti at Ca' d'Oro (*attrib.*)

Plate 176. VENUS BLINDFOLDING CUPID
Washington, National Gallery of Art (*attrib.*)

Plate 177. ST JEROME
Lugano, Thyssen Collection (*attrib.*)

Plate 178. CHRIST GIVING HIS BLESSING
Leningrad, Hermitage (*attrib*.)

Plate 179. ST MARY MAGDALENE
Naples, Capodimonte (*attrib.*)

Plate 180. ST·CATHERINE OF ALEXANDRIA
Boston, Museum of Fine Arts (*attrib.*)

Plate 181. CHRIST AND SIMON OF CYRENE
Leningrad, Hermitage (*attrib.*)

Plate 182. CHRIST ON THE CROSS AND THE GOOD THIEF
Bologna, Pinacoteca (*attrib.*)

Plate 183. ECCE HOMO
Madrid, Prado (*attrib.*)

Plate 184. THE MADONNA OF PITY
Florence, Pitti Palace (*attrib.*)

Plate 185. SPAIN COMING TO THE AID OF RELIGION
Rome, Doria Gellery (*attrib.*)

LOST PAINTINGS

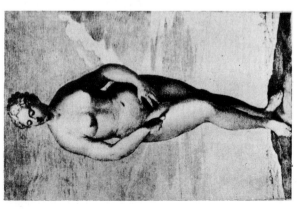

Plate 186. NUDE WOMAN
engraving by J. Piccini
and JUDITH
engraving by A. M. Zanetti

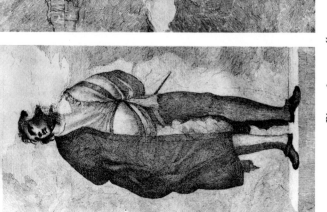

Plate 187. THE "COMPAGNO DELLA CALZA" *and* WOMENS' HEADS AND
BUST
engravings by A. M. Zanetti

Plate 188. ST PETER THE MARTYR
engraving by M. Rota

Plate 189. THE ANNUNCIATION
engraving by G. Caraglio

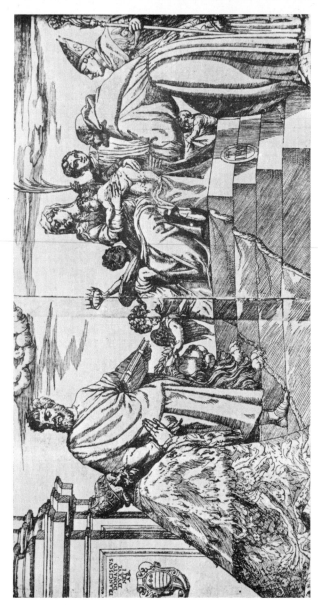

Plate 190. VOTIVE PORTRAIT OF THE DOGE ANDREA GRITTI
engraving by an unknown artist

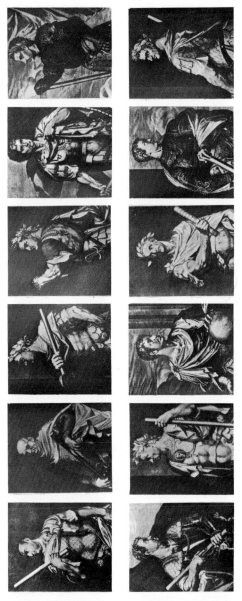

Plate 191. BUSTS OF ROMAN EMPERORS
engravings by E. Sadeler

Plate 192. THE BATTLE OF CADORE
copy, Florence

Plate 193. KING CHARLES V AND ISABELLA OF PORTUGAL
copy by Rubens, London

Plate 194. PORTRAIT OF JOHN FREDERICK OF SAXONY
copy, Madrid

Plate 195. TANTALUS
engraving by G. Sanudo

Plate 196. NOLI ME TANGERE
copy by A. Sanchez Coello, Madrid

Plate 197. ALLEGORY OF BRESCIA
drawing by Rubens, London
and THE FORGE OF THE CYCLOPS
engraving by M. Meier or C. Cort

Plate 198. ST PETER THE MARTYR
engraving by L. Bertelli